PERFORMING MUSIC

Performing Music

Shared Concerns

JONATHAN DUNSBY

CLARENDON PRESS · OXFORD

Oxford University Press, Walton Street, Oxford OX2 6DP

Oxford New York
Athens Auckland Bangkok Bombay
Calcutta Cape Town Dar es Salaam Delhi
Florence Hong Kong Istanbul Karachi
Kuala Lumpur Madras Madrid Melbourne
Mexico City Nairobi Paris Singapore
Taipei Tokyo Toronto

and associated companies in
Berlin Ibadan

Oxford is a trade mark of Oxford University Press

Published in the United States
by Oxford University Press Inc., New York

British Library Cataloguing in Publication Data
Data available

Library of Congress Cataloging in Publication Data
Dunsby, Jonathan.
Performing music : shared concerns / Jonathan Dunsby.
Includes bibliographical references (p.   ) and index.
1. Music—Performance. I. Title.
ML457.D86 1995 781.4'3—dc20 94–34885 CIP MN
ISBN 0–19–816642–7 (pbk.)

Typeset by Graphicraft Typesetters Ltd., Hong Kong
Printed in Great Britain
on acid-free paper by Bookcraft Ltd.
Midsomer Norton, Avon

Manuel Dunsby, MB, Ch.B.,
1920–1993

in memoriam

Acknowledgements

I OWE so much to such a large number of teachers, colleagues, students, and friends that this is the first of the 'impossible lists' of various kinds to which I refer from time to time in the following pages.

Those to whom I am grateful for expertise, encouragement, or both certainly include Eric Clarke, Lyn Jenkins, Penny Souster, John Stopford, and Anthony Storr.

I would like to thank those who have helped extensively, sometimes in long discussion at real cost to their own exceptionally valuable time, and I restrict this to those who commented on the entire manuscript. Nicholas Cook helped on general points and many details; James Ellis went to the heart of some spots of necessary rethinking; Kathleen Gibbons showed me how to consider step by step what the non-professional would need to understand, and also helped at low times with her zest for seeing things done; Jean-Jacques Nattiez cheered and cajoled (epistemologically) in equal measure; and Arnold Whittall, whose general influence on my ideas goes back many years to the time I became his junior colleague at King's College London, rooted out infelicities, and asked probing questions. I am especially grateful to Christopher Wilson, not only for his expert comments on the text itself, but also for the stimulus of our various joint teaching endeavours at the University of Reading in which a number of the arguments here were first thrashed out. As always, the author must take responsibility for whatever remains that may be questionable or actually inaccurate.

Finally, I record my ongoing dependence on the knowledge, intellect, taste, and dedication of my wife Esther Cavett-Dunsby. Unlike others mentioned here, she had to tolerate the hundreds of prior draft (and, I should think, occasionally daft) pages. She never said anything like 'it could be better', but just in her own quiet and persistent way repeatedly made it so with a word here, a big thought there.

J. M. D.

Jordans
April 1994

Contents

Introduction

I

Because for the first time in my publications I write deliberately in the first person, I begin with a story that seems to me to stamp the whole enterprise. 'Whole' is not written extravagantly, for after all this is a deliberately controlled number of pages, readable in one sitting by those who have the luxury of it, or in snatched time by busy students or people on commuter trains. The modern academic tendency to equate number of pages with extent of thought is something I do not claim to comprehend or find historical evidence for. My edition of Einstein's *Relativity* has 157 pages, in small format, and large print. To the story, however: before going up to Oxford a touch younger than most, a candidate had to have a special interview with the Warden of New College, Sir William Hayter. 'Do you think you will play a Bach Prelude and Fugue better', the Warden asked, 'for having done a music degree course?' The innocent reply was that this was something the candidate would like to find out.

Nowadays, I would simply say 'yes', provided that the playing is underpinned by sufficient talent, health, practice, nerve, intent, being in the right place at the right time, and whatever else universities do not claim to teach, but the centrality of which of course they recognize and encourage in as many ways as they can. When Philip Larkin was asked (now famously) how he had worked out the (admittedly brilliant) image of his poem 'Toads' (beginning 'Why should I let the toad *work* | Squat on my life?') and said that it was just 'genius', he was perpetuating an ivory-tower anti-intellectualism the benefit of which it is difficult to discern. Who says that Larkin's image of the toad is in any way 'better' than those flashes of inspiration that come to you and to me from time to time? It's doing something about it that matters or that, shall we say, is intended to endure. 'Doing something about it' is not the same as having the image, but it is what performers must always do.

II

I believe that there is a large community of people interested in what actually goes into performing Western music, although there are two fundamental hurdles in what I attempt here.

One is that performers vary so much in what concerns them, from a member of, say, Gothic Voices, the dedicated British group of singers who specialize in bringing medieval pieces to a wide audience, to the proverbial second violinist of a minor orchestra somewhere in deeply continental Europe, or perhaps the American mid-West, contemplating a one-hundredth participation in Tchaikovsky's Fifth Symphony and who, as they say, gave up music years ago, never having even thought about it if it was dated before about 1720, and hating it unreservedly if it was newish but not by Stravinsky.

The other hurdle is the vast spread of experience and knowledge, from dilettanti (which includes, of course, connoisseurs), and eager university 'performance option' Finals undergraduates, to Maestro So-and-so. I have no ambition to cope with the extremes but am convinced that there is a middle ground of shared concerns, where performers will forgive footnotes they are never going to follow up in a library, where researchers will forgive timely restatement of what they know, and where the lay reader will indulge that curiosity which led to this opening being read in the first place.

One never knows who may read a book, but my image of a readership has altered during the course of this work. I began with the idea of an academic study, learned in the sense of taking the most specialized possible view of the subject and making no concession in the way that ideas are expressed, even delighting in what is most abstruse (the French psychoanalytic author Lacan would have been, indeed has been elsewhere, my model of the writer who insists that it is precisely the almost insuperable difficulty of a text that makes it worth reading—the reader has to *earn* understanding, by the hardest possible work).

However, I have seen increasingly that this attitude, essential for some projects, can be counter-productive for other worthwhile tasks. The academic musician has a tough time defending academic music to other academics, although scientists seem to be much more sympathetic than colleagues in the Humanities. Where the real sympathy lies, however, is in the lay person, in people who simply enjoy music and find it an indispensable part of their lives. Rather than the grudging admission that there may be a certain skill and knowledge to writing about music, which one can sometimes wring out of fellow academics, among the general public I find an amazed admiration that someone can 'understand' music and musicians well enough to be in a position to comment upon them, upon the art and its artists.

Not only have I come to recognize how many people revere musicians of all kinds and don't put composers, performers, and writers in any form of destructive pecking order (see the discussion of 'doers' and 'talkers', pp. 47–8); but this realization has led me to take an interest in how musicians of a speculative, investigative turn of mind actually serve the public, or don't. I have been formidably influenced in this thinking by reading four books of the neurologist Oliver Sacks (*Awakenings, A Leg to Stand on, The Man Who Mistook His Wife for a Hat,* and *Seeing Voices*). I don't see how there could be a musical equivalent of these extraordinary journeys into the workings and in particular the dysfunctions of the human mind. What Sacks does demonstrate brilliantly, however, is that a book may truly serve more than one master. In his world in which both the professional and the lay reader can revel equally in the same text, and can benefit not only communally but also in entirely different ways from doing so, one feels that almost any bridge may be crossed. This is not at all the same issue as the issue many readers will have encountered in recent years, hearing those two so familiar questions, 'Have you read Stephen Hawking's *A Brief History of Time?*' (answer, very often, 'Yes'), 'And did you understand it?' (answer, very often and honestly, 'No'). With a certain patience and thought I would say that it is not possible *not* to understand Sacks, though the mysteries he describes may be, in the end, unfathomable. And that is an aspiration any of us may entertain in our own work without any want of humility and modesty.

'People who enjoy music' can surely enjoy reading about it. Despite the recent best efforts of such as Edward Said (*Musical Elaborations*) and Anthony Storr (*Music and the Mind*), people are not especially richly served in the current literature in this respect, and surely there is room for more— more that is different, and in particular about the activities of those musicians whom they most often observe at work, the performers. Indeed it must be that for most people the performer is the embodiment of music. More than likely they will never have met a composer, a musicologist, or an instrument maker—a piano tuner, perhaps, but even that highly skilled professional is increasingly less likely to be encountered than the microchip-replacer. Technology has not quenched the public thirst for live music, however, and it is often argued that music recorded in fact brings greater numbers of people to hear, to watch, to savour in every way the 'real thing'. It is this real thing in certain of its aspects that I hope will be found stalking these pages, a mere shadow of its actuality, no doubt, but omnipresent, the concern behind the concerns.

Musicians themselves are not well served, either, on the issues that will be aired here. For instance, a young musician who is contemplating hundreds of hours of practice a year over many years, and virtually every day if progress is not to be arrested, skills even lost, has every right to ask, 'What will it be like? What will I need to know? How will I learn to think about what I'll be doing?' and a host of similar questions. I suspect there are very few occasions when the individual teacher replies, 'Well I suggest you read this and that'. As I shall explain in the text, there is precious little 'this and that' to which we can turn, but I hope there will be a great deal more in the future. Alfred Brendel once wrote of his wish that some piano players might understand how they would be of greater service to music as piano technicians, servicing and tuning instruments. I would add that some musicologists might turn their exceptional intelligence to helping performers to understand better their activity, with its ideals and its fears as well as its practicalities. Obviously, I am not going to ask musicologists to perform, to say that if performers can retreat to important contemplative tasks, the contemplative professionals ought to leap into the glare of the spotlight and do something more conspicuous. What they can well do, however, and what is of practical help, happens in the teaching room, the rehearsal studio, and the dressing room. Sometimes, in all these places, it is drawn from the bookshelf. Why not? I have come upon all sorts of markers to show that performers do not tend to be interested in what is written. What I understand less is why those who write do not nevertheless seek on occasion to be read by performers. Performers are not an underclass. Far from it; if they're not sharp as nails, they won't go on for long, composers will be stumped, and there'll be nothing left to think about that might even remind us of Tchaikovsky's Fifth Symphony. Those who write can do a little sharpening.

III

In the first chapter I attempt to encapsulate my views on the relationship between making music and thinking, by exposing the fundamental role that chance plays in musical performance, and by weighing this against the fact that we are nevertheless constrained to 'pattern' the world. Chapter 2, as its title indicates, is about 'performance studies' in music, and I argue that although we need such a discipline, for training, for professionalism, for audiences' understanding, it hardly yet exists in the form that one day it might, following on from my hortatory words above. In Chapter 3 I turn from concepts to feelings, to what it feels like to perform music, and I take as starting-points not the customary idealized search for perfection, beauty, truth, and all the good that undoubtedly *is* what we aim for when making and experiencing music, but the realities of it—the difficulty of balancing instinct with intelligence, for instance, and the challenge of understanding 'artistry' in music, and 'mystery'.

Against this backdrop to establish why musical performance should need discussion, why music and word must be brought together, in Chapter 4 I look at some of the large trends in recent (published) thought about these matters, and not surprisingly this circles around the time-honoured poles of 'structure' on the one hand, 'effect' on the other. The 'Romantic legacy' studied in Chapter 5 reminds us that this is not an abstract debate, but cultural; we are all embedded in a musical world that, far from being uniform, shifts and snakes under the competing pressures of the past and the present. We need to be aware of this, or so I propose.

The two final chapters seek to explain musical sound and musical design, not in any full and final way, but in certain respects that I find striking and, it is hoped, relevant for the reader, from the point of view of performer and listener. As to sound, I aim to show that it is essentially a function of time. Casually, we tend to regard sound as the sort of thing-in-itself just like any other sensual impression; bask in it we do, but it is fascinating to contemplate what is going on as we bask. Not wanting to cloud the issue with metaphysical speculation, my exposition is of concrete examples, such as the 'balance' of musical sound, and even the 'concrete' *illusions* of musical texture. I go on to consider, in Chapter 7, how design brings sound to life, and how the performer has to 'animate' that design. A simple piece by Stravinsky (but what *is* 'simple'?) is examined for the kind of notated clues that a peformer needs, that a listener will appreciate. It almost goes without saying that a musical score has to be inter-preted. Every performer knows this and is taught it on the knee. The question is, if the performer somehow creates the music, what can we say about the constraints? Getting the right notes in the right order at about the right time is a good start, but I hope that the case-study gives an indica-tion of the work a performer might have to do and, let it be said, of what riddles will remain.

1

The Writer's Position

For a listener who wears earplugs, a very loud performance is the best.

(Jerrold Levinson)

Here I put forward basic ideas about what the musician is
probably doing. 'Probably' indicates that this is an earthy
outset, not a deliberately philosophical one. In my experience many people come to music without having had the
opportunity or encouragement to 'think through' what their
engagement with this art may mean. Perhaps for the listener
this is of no great moment, since life is too short to reflect
on sheer enjoyment, earplugs or no earplugs (I shall return
to this). Any technical entanglement with music, however,
all the way from getting a sense of what 'tonic' might mean
to mastering a Paganini *Caprice* on the violin, brings an
inevitable pondering. Musicians think hard. Whether 'think'
is quite the right word is debatable. We might prefer to say
that they ponder on what they do as musicians, 'ruminate'
and so on. The important point is that they do not usually
work in some sort of unreflecting musical trance.

It is not easy to convey to those few for whom music
holds no interest at all that 'thought' in its familiar sense is
integral to music. Such individuals are rare. If they weren't,
there would not be a vast popular music industry, and business and commerce would not pay such attention to background music, phone-hold music, and other customer-care
uses of music that most musicians themselves find repug-
nant. Most people do 'understand' music in that there is
always some kind of music they know they like, and with
this comes an intuitive understanding that music does not

happen by accident, that it is the product of the human mind. It requires skill to compose it, to perform it, to listen to it actively, fully concentrating, not merely dancing to its rhythms or swooning to its tunes.

Even for the lay person, music is part of 'thought', as the neurologist Sigmund Freud expressed succinctly: 'tunes that come into one's head without warning turn out to be determined by and to belong to a train of thought which has a right to occupy one's mind though without one's being aware of its activity'.[1] There is a world of difference, naturally, between happening to 'think' a tune and attending (and attending *to*) a long concert or opera. Yet even this 'happening' to think of a tune, Freud argues, shows that music belongs to the very fabric of thought just like numbers and their computation, or like visualizations. There is a great deal more to human thought than words, vital though true 'language' is to our functioning as normal human beings. And though specialists will surely continue to disagree on quite how it works in all its aspects, few would contend that performing music does not result in some form of communication.

Internally, as it were, thinking hard comes so naturally to those engaged in music that often they don't see it for what it is. Partly this is because musicians are aware, perhaps exceptionally aware, of the forces at work in the unconscious mind (or whatever it is 'correct' to call that part of our mental activity which we know is going on, but cannot *summon*). Many performers experience the fact that learning and performing a new piece of music does not happen all at once. The first performance, as good as it may be, is not as satisfying as the second, and—though I can prove this only anecdotally—it is the third performance where magically everything seems to come together. 'Magically' perhaps, an idea that will arise several times again in our discussion of performing music, but it is so familiar that musicians take it to be, as it is, an everyday process. What is going on in

---

[1] *Introductory Lectures on Psychoanalysis*, trans. James Strachey (Harmondsworth: Penguin, 1973), 138.

the mind in those two gaps that may be hours apart or months? Clearly it is some kind of unconscious thinking, often called 'assimilation', though this is simply a naming of something, not an analysis of it. I would add, almost parenthetically, that children who are schooled towards one single examination or audition performance of a piece of music which is then dropped in the quest for new repertoire are being deprived of one of the most significant aspects of musical learning, unconscious assimilation following performance 'peaks'.

Not seeing it 'for what it is' is also a function, however, of the habits of the mind rather than the mysteries of its deep recesses. There is an array of perfectly comprehensible conceptual problems confronting the musician—just like the lawyer, the doctor, the priest, and the poet—and I believe it is because they are constantly in play that they are not often thought about. Thus taken for granted, they can be viciously troubling when things go wrong. A very common example is when the performer takes on a task that over-stretches conceptual ability, a 'difficult' piece of music, perhaps because the harmony is very complex, or because it involves a text that is refractory in its 'meaning', or even because it is not in fact all that well composed and involves inherent structural weaknesses. The emotional result for the performer may be undue nervousness, a level of tension that serves to degrade performance rather than enliven it. At the least there will be a lack of satisfaction in the music-making, and the listener will surely pick this up—earplugs or not. What is interesting about the three common causes just mentioned is that they are susceptible to similar solutions: they are cases where an improved *theoretical* understanding of the music, harnessed of course to talent and physical self-discipline, will without doubt help; and theoretical understanding is thinking just like any other thinking. I shall return to this general subject in Chapter 7.

As to those earplugs, I certainly don't mean to be frivolous about them. The quotation at the head of this chapter is from the work of a respected American philosopher (whom

I am nevertheless going to take to task in Chapter 2!).[2] It has the characteristics of a memorable aphorism: while catching our attention through the humour of the absurd, it also encapsulates an important slice of life, a truth rather than a truism. Levinson's idea, for all that he is cited out of context and thus a little unfairly, is to articulate the very contingency, dependence on *chance*, of musical communication, and this is not any sort of dull relativism. I would say that, above all, it is just realistic. This will speak to the heart of every practising musician—practising in both normal senses of the word. Albeit the preparation of the performer has been done to perfection, every technical problem mastered, every item of historical information duly weighed in the balance, every expressive nuance felt through to a condition of complete conviction, every theoretical aspect considered in due measure, what you cannot do is take account of the member of the audience who is wearing earplugs for a reason that will never be known. That is the listener you *cannot* prepare for or deal with at all.

This is to say much more than (to misquote Abraham Lincoln) 'you cannot please all the people all of the time'. There are many fundamentally contingent aspects to music-making of all kinds; although the performer can seek to eliminate some uncertainties, there will always be others. Indeed, much commercial music and modern 'classical' electronic music has demonstrated—not that musicians didn't always know it—that what is wholly predictable is artistically lifeless. There are so many ways to examine contingency that 'chance in music' can itself be the subject of a long disquisition, which is not my intention. To pin it down as one element of a wider picture, I can do no better than to comment on musical sound itself, and even then only briefly at this point (see Chapter 6).

The jury is still out on whether the digital sound of a CD, with its mathematically exact values, is artificial compared with the rich messiness of an analogue recording (be it on a

---

[2] See below, p. 26.

wax or an LP). Yet acousticians have known for decades that those sounds perceived to be the most interesting and artistically satisfying are the sounds that appear to be the least simple mathematically when analysed. The searing heights of Jascha Heifetz's E string will always look like a complete mess when broken into frequency distributions on the oscilloscope—the violin, totem of beauty in modern Western musical culture, is exceptionally 'impure' acoustically.

Contingency, and illusion, can be heard non-experimentally by anyone who cares to attend a virtuosic piano recital in a large hall that has a 'wet' acoustic, that is, lots of echo. Listen to the actual quality of sound very high up the register of the Steinway Model D, their large concert grand piano, especially in rapid passage-work, brilliantly executed because it is so evenly spaced: coolly assessed by the conscious ear, it is arguably a series of rapid 'mechanical' knocks more than it is a shape of musical notes, though normally what the listener hears and wants to hear is the notes themselves, just as in the tenor and soprano registers. Anyone, I believe, can hear the knocking, once it is drawn to the attention. Conversely I have yet to meet or read of anyone, including those who attend to these things carefully with an expert ear, who claims to be able to perceive a 'knock' of any kind in the initial luminous sound of the vibrating string lower down the register of an excellent concert grand piano. If this were truly a problem, that is if there were a general problem of *perceived* gross impurity in the sound of the piano, composers since Beethoven would have composed differently. In other words, the presence (high up) or absence (lower down) of 'knocking' *doesn't matter* musically because we pattern it out.

It might be argued that the aesthetic pleasure to be taken in things that 'work' correctly, be it a musical structure or a mathematical proof, is in fact the aspiration of creative minds whether musical or scientific, over long centuries of Western societies, and in other societies too. I do not deny this terrific urge to try to make things work correctly, which one sees in all fields of human endeavour. 'Man is', as Leonard

Meyer writes in *Music, the Arts, and Ideas*, a book that has shaped the thinking of successive generations of musicians, 'perhaps above all else, a *predicting* animal. . . . He must pattern the world. Indeed, were this not the case, man would have long since gone the way of the dinosaurs . . .'[3] We *must* pattern the world, is the lesson we learn from the behavioural sciences.

If it is in our nature to tend to see improvement as accomplishment, applause as approval, status as reality, and all the examples that could be offered of how we are driven to 'fix' behaviour, to endow it with permanent *value*, nevertheless a moment's reflection reminds us that just as nothing is permanent, so nothing is perfect, not even a Mozart symphony; at least, not if you listen to it wearing earplugs, which is to say rather obviously that there is no 'perfect' musical audience, let alone a perfect executant bringing to life a perfect piece of music. Here we may appear to have a conundrum. You go to perform as best you can, but you don't know what you are supposed to be dealing with. Or you are a receiver—listener, consumer, audience—but you cannot know what you will get. In other words, *music is always a risk*, for everyone, all the time.

However, I think it is important to stress from the beginning of this enquiry that studying music is no less 'scientific' than studying science itself, than that hotbed of theories, mishaps, and constant improvement that is the index of previous failure; and one could, indeed should equally well say that science is no less artistic than music.[4] This does not mean, however, that striving towards a goal is in fact pointless merely because of the inevitable contingency of things. What Lincoln actually did say or is claimed to have said in

---

[3] (Chicago: University of Chicago Press, 1967), 227–8.

[4] Lewis Wolpert argues against 'the idea that arts and sciences are basically similar in that they are both creative products of the human imagination'. He says that this is true 'only at a relatively low level'. But he also admits that 'it is no use for anyone to pretend that there is, at present, any real understanding of the creative process in any human activity', and thus one rather loses confidence in his position on this point. See *The Unnatural Nature of Science* (London: Faber and Faber, 1992), 56–8.

a speech in 1858 will be well known to most readers: 'You can fool all the people some of the time, and some of the people all the time, but you cannot fool all the people all of the time'. That is not just an abiding political observation, but a pointer to the musician or would-be musician at any level that there really is some grist in the mill. There is *judgement*—what people think.

We see with our own eyes and hear with our own ears only *transient* effects of human judgement, only those ideas more or less now in fashion. This is because we live for a relatively short time, in the sense that we are each descended from a direct line of thousands of generations of next of kin, yet only one, two, perhaps three, four at a pinch of these generations can ever have met. The profound grip of human judgement on our aspirations is nevertheless constantly in evidence in the historical traces it leaves. The listener 'wearing earplugs' may have been the one person in whose hands once lay some profound choices, to the effects of which we are now subject, not knowing why. (In a curious sort of way, in Chapter 4 I shall be able to name him and the trouble he caused, though I shall do this reverently as one certainly must in the case of Beethoven.) For the musical performer this transience has a special quality, shared with other arts such as acting (which will also arise again here) and dance: there is no *record* of its ancestry. We may know for a 'fact' that that Thracian troubadour Orpheus was given to rendering wild beasts spellbound by his lyre playing, but his lyricism is gone for all time. The past is *silent*. It is interesting to ask whether technology, in its sound recording, then vision and sound, holography, virtual reality, and who knows what may come next, is generating a fundamental shift in this situation. We may be witnesses, the only direct witnesses there will ever be, to the beginning of the music of the future. Is it not easy to imagine that two thousand years or five thousand from now people will say that Western music really only got going properly during the twentieth century from which distant time there date the earliest proper sonic and visual records, following that strange 'mute' early period of music history that spanned the Greeks (of which we know essentially nothing), via medieval polyphony (of which we know a certain amount), to, say, Mahler, the last great pre-technological composer (of whose work and times we know much more but not, really, enough: none of his performances survive recorded, and there are just memories mythically handed on to indicate that he was one of the greatest-ever conductors)?

To sum up, in what follows I shall attempt as musicians do to steer a course between the Scylla and Charybdis that we have now espied in the distance—between the devouring monster of human *judgement*, and the whirlpool that threatens to engulf all artistic certainties in the frothing sea of *contingency*. Once again and finally I stress that this is not a philosophical position. It is a workable basis for action that I put forward as appropriate to the mind of the performer: a double awareness, of 'what people seem to think' and of 'what may conceivably happen'. The reader may protest 'but I am an artist, and my only guide must be what *I* think' or, as a listener, 'but I thought all that matters, artist, is that you—as Shakespeare put it—to thine own self be true'! It would be an understandable protest, to be considered more specifically in Chapter 3. Meanwhile, the workable basis stands. It is, I contend—and as promised at the beginning of this chapter, 'what the musician is probably doing'.

2

Musical Performance Studies as a 'Discipline'

> Read not to contradict and confute, nor to believe and take for granted, nor to find talk and discourse, but to weigh and consider.
>
> (Francis Bacon, 'Of Studies', *Essays or Counsels, Civil and Moral*)

I trot out the term 'discipline' of musical performance studies as if it clearly existed, but it is as well to state that this term at present stands merely for 'subject' or 'topic'. 'Discipline' carries the implication of a received body of knowledge and an orderliness in whatever is conducted in its name, however subversively. I shall repeatedly comment on the fact that this does not really seem to have been the case in musical performance studies.

The latest copy of *Répertoire International de Littérature Musicale*, the beating heart of music research which provides abstracts of anything it can find that has been published anywhere in the world, retains the classification 'Performance Practice and Notation', now of more than two decades' standing. It may be right to do so, but the term 'performance practice', to the living generation of academic musicians who are aware of these niceties, has a somewhat fusty feel to it. True, without the legacy of the 'performance practice' tradition of the nineteenth and twentieth centuries we would not be in a position to do various important things: for instance, to play from good editions that provide a musical text in which reasonable trust can be placed; or to refer to old treatises on interpretation that give us a picture of what musicians thought in days gone by when the music we are playing originated.

I would like to insist, then, that anyone who chooses to deride that discipline of 'performance practice' recognized by *RILM* is on the wrong track. Performance practice very often *has* been chided, mostly for its dissociation from musical 'real life'. Even more to the point for our discussion, it is widely *ignored* in the investigations of general musicology. It is quite an indication of this that in one of the most recent authoritative essays, Peter Williams's 'Performance Practice Studies', with only a few exceptions there is no reference to the opinion-formers of modern musicology;[1] and I do not record this to criticize Williams, but to point to the difficulty he would have faced in trying to trawl general musical thought for *distinctive* ideas about performance studies.

Yet there *is* a broader idea nowadays of performance studies viewed from the position of the performer. The performer may say, 'well, what is my position?', and I aim to keep that question in mind throughout these pages. It is a question reflecting the spirit of the times, and it is hardly necessary for me to quote from an extensive list of sources of comment on this in recent years from players, critics, historians, and theorists. They all tend to subscribe to the one climate of opinion, that performers need a *frame of reference* for how they think about music in general, and for how they go about their training and their job or pastime.

Musical performance has customarily been a prerequisite for and a component of tertiary music education, and this aspect of performance studies is a convenient starting-point for a consideration of the range and nature of the subject. The customary polarization in the United Kingdom of 'university' music with its emphasis on scholarly tasks, and 'music college' training heavily weighted towards practical work, is

---

[1] In *Companion to Contemporary Music Thought*, ed. J. Paynter *et al.* (London: Routledge, 1992), 931–47. By leading 'opinion-formers' I mean such as Dahlhaus, Kerman, Mellers, and Nattiez, who form a combined and generally agreed backdrop to 'contemporary musical thought', invidious though it is to try to name names, thus not naming others.

beginning to soften. If in the UK it is a 'polarization', in continental Europe it may be called a strict separation. It is becoming increasingly evident world-wide, however, that considerable factual knowledge is needed in order to perform music effectively. To take the most obvious example, the more an authenticist approach becomes to the taste of audiences and of professional 'fixers' (agents and so on), the more important it is for the student to learn to research the historical and stylistic aspects of different repertoires which will, in the end, allow professional standards to be attained and maintained, and personal artistry to flower. This tendency towards the recognition of the need for *knowledge*, which has grown so strikingly in respect of the mainstream repertoire, has never been less than glaringly obvious in the study of twentieth-century music, which in its sheer diversity offers a challenge to the performer's ability to assimilate different notations, different techniques, and more recently different technologies. Conversely—and for all that I would defend the role of pure musical scholarship to the hilt—young musicians are no longer taught that the academic study of music should be, or can be, divorced from practical concerns. Beyond an emphasis on listening, music is regarded as something to be performed (and, of course, composed), so that for example the dry university music syllabus of former decades is no longer acceptable: performance studies are well-nigh universally built into music education of all types.

Evidently, given the two poles of what I am saying, about what is happening, and about what is being done about what is happening, *practice has run ahead of theory* in these developments, and it is not easy for the young musician to gain the insight and information needed to underpin the sheer physical work that leads to practical accomplishment (this is to return to one of the themes of my Introduction). Though there is no way to demonstrate it—or certainly no way that I know of—one cannot but suspect that many musicians at the start of a career, or of a lifetime of recreational music-making, do not feel particularly confident, competent, qualified, or secure. It would be futile to search for a simple formula to improve this situation, but it is my belief that there has been a lack of airing of the issues in common which those learning to play Western music are bound to have to face.

A plausible reason for the slender development of a performers' literature is that music in modern Western society is bewilderingly diverse, as is readily outlined in a contemplation of the fallacy as to why new music is supposedly problematic. While contact between the public and new music has been said, countless times, to be something virtually lost and possibly deliberately abandoned in the twentieth century (the so-called deliberation being an offence of composers, not the public), it has to be remembered that the number of listeners has grown vastly during this period of supposed alienation. I do not know that the total audience for Wagner in, say, the 1860s has ever been calculated even very roughly, but taking into account all performances, and every act of access to printed vocal scores among educated Europeans and Americans, would the figure reach one million? Compare that—whatever the answer within the bounds of reasonableness—with the audience for a Britten opera on television in the UK a century later. The million is already exceeded on one occasion for what, with all due respect to Britten, is a relatively minor cultural event in comparison with the world's exposure to Wagner between the years 1860 and 1870.

Further, if there has been a tendency to exaggerate grossly the supposed gulf between the public and new music (what comparable public has *ever* been in contact before with its new music?), this exaggeration has been fed by the very novelty of the phenomenon of the dissemination of classical music among a new public, and of the well-nigh universal dissemination of popular music—Beethoven's Ninth is, we might want to assert, quite well embedded in certain corners of Western culture, but McCartney's 'Yesterday' is known to billions of human beings, literally, and significantly—it is the sign of a world-wide lingua franca. Moreover, 'old' music has come to embrace further and further reaches back into the Western repertoire, and this too stretches the very basis of the concept 'music'. Those who have struggled to develop a taste for and understanding of the European and American avant-garde have a relatively new circle of fellow sufferers, the disseminators of so-called early music, medieval music in particular; and as is well known in other disciplines the challenges of modern art may often seem rather small when compared with the extraordinary complexities—and artistic achievements—of the medieval mind.

I am not arguing that the evident diversity of what is called music—ethnic issues not even having been considered here—is solely at the heart of the poverty in performance studies. Plausible that diversity may be as a reason, because it is so easy to point to; but deeper in societal mechanisms, I believe, is the inherent *change* at the sharp edge of musical culture, that is, in the rendition of music.

Although I have taken education as a starting-point, it would be wrong to imply that learning is a task only for the young. In the course of a normal lifetime (and although I have said that a lifetime is a rather brief phenomenon historically), cultural changes do occur that to a greater or lesser extent demand, if not retraining, then at the least some reassessment of the individual's knowledge and skills (and thus everything to be said in this book is addressed to the reader regardless of his or her *age*, a factor I have not yet mentioned).

Performance practice inevitably evolves, sometimes with radical consequences. For instance, in the eighteenth century there was no such profession as the opera producer, that nowadays seemingly indispensable and all-powerful figure. There was essentially no such profession left in the nineteenth century as the continuo player, even though the eighteenth-century musician would have been stunned to learn of a proximate future when orchestras would play without harpsichords, and when keyboard accompaniment would in any case become fully notated with no opportunity for embellishment and improvisation. In the early twentieth century, to earn a living playing the sackbut, precursor of the trombone, had been an impossibility of some two hundred years' standing, and who would have guessed that it might become possible again in 'early music' groups of the 1990s?

What is true of the central, actual music-making practices I have just mentioned, holds true at the halo, in musical commentary. To take a very recent example, even if Hans Keller did not succeed in persuading all critics, and all other phoney professionals as he called them, to cease their activity,[2] the late 1980s did bring a sea-change in the relationship between the press and musical performance, when the previously endemic overnight 'what I thought of the concert' type of newspaper review became suddenly unfashionable, no longer regarded as politically correct. Of course, in this particular little shift in musical life we have seen another fallacy at work. Whatever is wrong with an overnight review, phoned in breathlessly to a newspaper copy desk shortly after the end of a concert, is equally wrong when the critic's fax hums in copy to the newspaper some hours later. The result is still 'news' to the newspaper reader, and culture is still cheapened in the way that Karl Kraus and Thomas Mann (to name two notables among many) wrote of nearly a century ago. All the same, there *has* been a change of practice, of appearance, in the recent past; and this is the point I wanted to make.

Gathering together the threads from above, we know, if it is accepted, that performance studies are part of the mainstream itself of musical learning, but that they are ineluctably fluid and, when examined in the present or recent past, liable to apparently *erratic* evolution. Obviously then—and it is hardly a revelation—we are dealing with something that is of real importance while also being extremely difficult to pin down. Thus there is a challenge to be taken on. This is not to say that fine musical minds have not been applied to

---

[2] See *Criticism* (London: Faber and Faber, 1987). The reader who has not had the opportunity to absorb this lucid, entertaining, and enlightening book may be encouraged to do so if I list Keller's phoney musical professions—viola player, opera producer, conductor, music critic, musicologist—and 'other phoney professions'—broadcaster, editor, politician, psychoanalyst, psychiatrist, teacher (pp. 17–80). There is often a real sense of fun in Hans Keller's writings, but always to a deadly serious end.

worthwhile questions over the centuries. As I have said, however, little sense has emerged of a discipline, or even just a broad field of studies in which it is possible to claim that at least the obvious has been tackled effectively. For fear of pursuing this point in such abstract terms as to approach a void, I offer two concrete examples of the kind of problem I have in mind.

The first case is discussions of performance practice in the music of Mozart that have appeared in the prestigious journal *Early Music*, and in particular the set of essays which adopts a music-analytical attitude to the identification and solution of questions of interpretation—that is, it looks to internal evidence in the music's structure as opposed to historical, extra-musical information. The entire enterprise is introduced by an essay from James Webster, the eminent American musicologist. His reader is encouraged to welcome analytical approaches and is promised that 'just as form and expression are the dialectically related poles of coherence in any artwork, so an ideal or comprehensive musical understanding is possible only when one relates structure and context, immanent and generic content'.[3] Now what is the unwary performer, whether student, professional, or amateur likely to make of this claim? Translated into more or less ordinary language (though it is not the language but the point itself to which I object), what Webster says is that it is possible to conquer all doubts and curiosities about music given sufficient intellectual and historical legwork. I think he is claiming that you really can master Mozart's music, deal with it, command it, *solve* it.

With little or no knowledge of the analytical literature— and music analysis *is* a discipline, which has been conducted in an atmosphere of energetic, informed debate—one can only believe it or not. Yet the non-specialist reader is likely to be honestly sceptical, as we all tend to be when confronted with blanket statements about the application of

[3] 'Analysis and the Performer: Introduction', *Early Music*, 20/4 (Nov. 1991), 591.

supposedly absolute truths. That would in fact be quite right, since Webster, no doubt in a genuine attempt to be persuasive and helpful to the lay observer, has suppressed all indication of how controversial his position is in the first place. Among music theorists and analysts a clear correspondence between analytical 'interpretation' and actual musical performance is widely doubted.[4] Why this is so, what it may imply, what may be learned from the situation, all remains hidden because, as I said above, the obvious has not been tackled. Performers know about 'form' in the sense that they know it helps to be aware where they are in a piece when playing it (see Chapter 7 for closer discussion of this). They will also have some personal conception of what 'expression' means, that is, they will have an *attitude*, be it 'this will come over well if I just do what I've been trained to do', or 'I have to pour unrequited love into bar 100 and not forget a touch of fear and loathing at bar 210', or 'this woman conducts the orchestra very well and I'd better play precisely as she is showing me how to'. But what on earth is an *'ideal or comprehensive musical understanding'*? It is my contention that this is where the performer parts company with the scholar, not because the problem is not a constant concern, but because it is put in an unhelpfully unrealistic way.

The second case illustrates this more generally. The source here is Peter le Huray's *Authenticity in Performance: Eighteenth-Century Case Studies*, its own second case-study being a fascinating investigation into aspects of the first Prelude of the second book of J. S. Bach's *Das wohltemperierte Clavier*.[5] I have no complaint at all about the helpful contents of the nineteen pages in question, the virtuous subtitles of which speak for themselves: 'on choosing a good edition', 'fingering as evidence of performance style', 'Bach's keyboard instruments', 'phrasing and articulation', and 'analysis as an interpretative tool'.

[4] One statement on this is my own article 'Analysis and Performance', *Music Analysis*, 8/1–2 (1989).
[5] (Cambridge: Cambridge University Press, 1990), ch. 2, 'Bach's C Major Prelude BWV 870 and 870A', 5–23.

On the contrary, what speaks loudest here is not what is present, with which one may take issue here and there in the way that professionals do, but what is missing. Why, the performer will surely ask, should these topics be studied? What benefit is foreseen from this patient endeavour? How does it help, for instance, to be told that Bach's piece is probably best performed, and thus listened to, on the clavichord, an instrument of 'transparent, clearly articulated sounds' that 'encouraged a performance of great expressive clarity' (p. 13)? These are not rhetorical questions. There is a real, pragmatic issue. The performer is invited to take the time to contemplate something that I at least find ultimately vacuous, however well intended. To put it baldly, I have not the least conception of what 'expressive clarity' is supposed to mean in this context. In an informal sense I suppose that we all know roughly what le Huray seeks to convey, but that is not good enough for those who are taking the time to study his work, actively *choosing* not to do something else. How does it help to be told of a quality, 'expressive clarity', which formally stated surely amounts to nothing more than, say, 'good playing', whatever *that* means. What's more, assuming I have some private conception of what 'expression' means, this will be informed by—it will depend upon—the instruments on which I have been trained or have been used to listening to. While I wouldn't wish to deny any player or listener the freshening experience of the clavichord, it will remain a kind of dabbling if introduced into our consciousness in the informal, superficially open-minded spirit adopted by le Huray.

The idea of 'good playing' takes us even closer to the nexus of this part of the discussion, and allows me to return to the sentence quoted at the head of Chapter 1, which of course cannot be left explained only as an example of contingency and toyed with a bit in the narrative.

My two cases have exemplified what it is like in performance studies when even preliminary matters are not addressed thoroughly, that is, usefully. I think I can demonstrate this problem acutely at what might be deemed the highest level, philosophically. Levinson's sentence, it seems to me, is not a serious proposition (nor intended as such) but an example of how there must be more than one perspective in evaluating a performance: there is no 'transcendental' category for this.[6] It is an important prop in the main thesis of this philosopher's essay, 'Evaluating Musical Performance':

The question 'Is performance *P* of work *W* a good one, and if so, how good?' can generally receive no *single* answer, but only a *series* of answers, for specifications of the question to various musically legitimate individuals, positions, contexts, and purposes.[7]

Is it not cause for surprise that it was necessary, or thought necessary by a respected professional, to conduct such an argument in 1990? Do we really not recognize a 'good' performance, and do we almost to this day need to be told through philosophical argument that there is no 'best' performance? Although Levinson's argument in the essay is handsomely constructed and a real pleasure to pore over if you are interested in that sort of thing, I fail to discover in it anything of substance that had not been said eloquently more than four decades ago, by Roger Sessions (and here I am simply turning to the most obvious, easily obtainable, well-known source):

Music is by its very nature subject to constant renewal, and the performer is not in any sense either a mere convenience or a necessary evil. By the same token, the idea of the 'ideal' or even in any strict sense the 'authoritative' performance is an illusory one. The music is not totally present, the idea of the composer is not fully expressed, in any single performance, actual or even conceivable, but rather in the sum of all possible performances. But having admitted this, we are bound to insist also that the number of possible performances is limited by the composer's text and by the musical intentions which that text embodies.[8]

---

[6] *Music, Art, and Metaphysics* (Ithaca, NY: Cornell University Press, 1990), 382.

[7] Ibid. 392. The essay was originally published in a journal in 1987.

[8] *The Musical Experience of Composer, Performer, Listener* (Princeton, NJ: Princeton University Press, 1971), 85.

I do not want to adopt or sustain a highly critical stance towards the literature of performance studies, in whatever sense it is practicable to claim that there is a literature of the field. These were just emblematic cases that have struck me as, each in a different way, likely to induce pessimism, possibly despair, in anyone venturing into an area that I have already characterized as difficult, but important, and central to music-making. I think they show us *types*—overstatement, understatement, post-statement—for which we should be on guard in the search for stimulus and development in performance studies.[9]

The reader may be assured that there are some fascinating texts that any performer would enjoy and benefit from studying, and some of these will be introduced in each chapter here. I have not so much as mentioned yet the large 'how to' category of writing about performance which we all inevitably come across if only in the pedagogical tutors, rudimentary to advanced, in different instruments and in musical general knowledge. This printed passing on of craft and fact down the generations is a wonder to behold in music stores around the world. Musical pedagogy overall has a splendid track record: it is because music *has* been taught from generation to generation that it has been able to thrive and evolve. However, that is more to do with how we *learn* music, and this is not a subject that I care to weave, distractingly (and elongatingly), into these considerations of how we *do* it, and observe it being done.

What I am trying to convey is not, then, a dismal scene, but a fragmentary one, in which there is a relatively random scattering of performance studies, sometimes lurking in written endeavours aimed at quite different ends, in which performance practice which figured briefly at the beginning of this chapter plays its essential part, but it is only a part. I hope to have put over that we do not have, as I said above, 'a received body of knowledge and an orderliness in whatever

[9] I recognize that the chances of any reader finding my own pages free of over-, under-, and post-statement, and perhaps lots more problems besides, are nil. I hope to have made it clear that this is not the point.

is conducted in its name, however subversively'. *Why* we do not have this is a tricky question that would require a full historical argument even to begin to answer. But as Gustave Reese predicted in the late 1960s, 'the practical and the scholarly branches of music are going to be thrown together more and more'.[10] He was right. It has been a relentless trend, if slow to develop: *Performing Music* is indeed one of its manifestations.

[10] 'Perspectives and Lacunae in Musicological Research' in (eds.), B. S. Brook *et al. Perspectives in Musicology* (New York: Norton, 1975), 1–14 (p. 11).

3

Anxiety and Artistry

> You'd be surprised how hard it can often be to translate
> an action into an idea.
>
> (Karl Kraus, *Half-Truths and One-and-a-Half Truths*)

The Western musical performer, in the modern world, is often in an uneasy state of mind, and I propose to explore here reasons for this, and what it may amount to in actuality.

Many writings in what may broadly be called the aesthetics of music ignore musical anxiety and elaborate instead on the deep artistic satisfaction to be found in music, on its capacity to preoccupy the mind, rid it of words, and put in their place a passage of time filled with a different, unique 'language'. This is what I call the Ecstasy school of musical thought.[1] It is something that most of us take for granted, having been taught that music is inherently good for us, which we find repeatedly confirmed in our experience of it, and confirmed intellectually for many on the grounds that it is extremely hard—perhaps impossible—to conjure up any substantial idea of a music that is in and of itself harming.

Ecstasy, from the Greek meaning 'to put out of place', is quite the word for an image of music that centres on its 'transports', on the way it seizes the mind and, during its course, frees the mind from all other conceptual work. It is

[1] I put the term ecstasy forward as an informal word that will be well understood. Musicologists will know that the 'heart and brain in music' debate has been up and running for centuries. Modern neurology is beginning to show that this is not an argument to be conducted between people so much as a division of attention present in *each* of us, though I suspect this has always been known. See Anthony Storr, *Music and the Mind* (London: Harper Collins, 1992). Philosophers will know that *ecstasis* is familiar in the early 20th-c. work of Martin Heidegger, and in Nietzsche's earlier discussion of platonic 'rapture'.

even beginning to be realized, in the field of music therapy, that music has a measurable, clinical effect on the human cortex. *The Times* of 15 October 1993 reported that 'All over the country, therapy units are popping up with the aim of alleviating every ill through music. Now we learn that a study at the University of California shows that listening to music can increase our intelligence'.

It is worth pursuing this thinking a little further in order to introduce the points below where I shall be relying on the Ecstasy school as a backdrop to the extreme difficulties that may arise 'in practice', as I noted above. Those absolutes about the goodness of music are so familiar to us that they may go entirely unchallenged and lead to an impoverished understanding of what making music is about in a full, rounded sense. It is all too easily forgotten, for instance, that in the Greek philosophical foundations of our modern societies the arts in general were considered problematic. In *The Republic*, Plato argues at great length about the proper place of art in society: indeed most of that book is devoted to this question. Equally, early on in Aristotle's extensive enquiry *Ethics* the philosopher makes it abundantly clear that there can be no analogy between music and virtue.[2] Nowadays, as always previously, there are customs, rites, and religions in which music is forbidden because of its various perceived dangers. There is, indeed, music of war—incantations, drummings, and so on specifically intended to transport the mind for harmful purposes. And there is even musical pathology: Oliver Sacks recounts the story of one patient suffering from a form of musicogenic epilepsy who complained, 'I can't use *my* songs. Anyhow, I'm tired of them—they're always the same. Musical hallucinations may have been a gift to Shostakovich, but they are only a nuisance to me. *He* didn't want treatment—but I want it badly'. Which of us has not said 'I just can't get that tune out of my head'?[3]

---

[2] See e.g. the widely available Penguin edition of *The Ethics of Aristotle*, trans. J. A. K. Thomson (Harmondsworth, 1983), 97.

[3] *The Man who Mistook his Wife for a Hat* (London: Pan Books, 1986), 135. In *Music, Imagination, and Culture* (Oxford: Oxford University Press,

I am not going to argue that we should develop some sort of Cautionary school of musical discourse to counteract the Ecstatics, but I am convinced that an idealistic approach to music-making *can* be a blinkered one that is of no use to either the professional or the amateur. There is mystery in music, but still a great deal that needs to be demystified.

We might begin to appreciate this by considering the differences between music and sport, and in particular the fact that musicians and their audiences are so suspicious of what is often described as 'theorizing'. In stark contrast, no normal sporting competitor has ever, surely, refused to listen to the latest physical or psychological theory. Anything that may enhance speed, strength, even gracefulness, is duly considered, the only burden of decision being whether it will be effective, offering a balance of benefit over jeopardy. In sport, there is *competition*, not only immediately, but in many cases measured against previous human performance, and in a sense the musician also competes against predecessors. It is not only that 'I know this has been done before but it is worth doing again, for music is a living art'; but also, 'I know *how* it came out before, and I am driven to do it either better or at least in a new way' (see below, Ch. 4 n. 1, which mentions the well-documented idea of 'anxiety of influence').

Now, evidently I cannot carry the contrast with sport too far before encountering serious objections. The distinction between game and art is not absolute, being almost non-existent in some cultures, and significantly blurable in our own. On the side of sport, there is always a level beyond clinical matters, where no one knows what produces the extra microsecond that may separate one athlete from another

1990) Nicholas Cook describes imagining music and states that this ' "hearing" is very different from what it would be like to hear the music in real life, for instance if someone suddenly switched on a radio in the next room' (p. 86). I am sure he is right, yet true musical hallucination is by all accounts precisely as if someone had switched on a radio. I know a number of musicians, myself included, and there are accounts of this in memoirs, diaries, and other documentary sources, who have dreamed music that is utterly vivid, indistinguishable from the real experience itself of listening to music, though usually difficult or impossible to recall on waking. When it is recalled, it is in the different, out-of-time, 'imagined' state described by Cook.

when both are way ahead of the field and ahead of normal, untrained human performance. At that level superstition is rife just as it is in the musical world. In the 1980s, mass culture captured an idea of it—not quite a sporting one— that spoke to millions who understood perfectly what was signified by the idea of a world, not ours, that it is given to few to inhabit: 'The Right Stuff'.

These comments are in place not to deny sport its mysterious aspects, but to provide by analogy some everyday confidence in the thought that when it comes to music, there is always a level *below* the mysterious, where plain lessons can be easily understood and eagerly learned, as will be exposed in Chapter 7. Staying with the analogy between sport and music, however, which analogy is acutely evident in their common performing or one might say 'motor' aspects, there is a recent and interesting contribution from one to the other, a popular import from sport-think entitled *The Inner Game of Music*.[4] Scholarly musicians will wince at the mere mention of this publication, for although being a successful product in the market to which it is addressed, it perpetuates mindless musical truisms, no doubt unintentionally, but causing turbulent distraction to the thoughtful reader. I choose almost at random as a taster: 'The performer, after all, can only *play what he hears . . .*' (p. 19, my emphasis). There could be a dissertation-length critique of those utterly misleading words—and a long one at that if it came from a feminist music aesthetician with a strong background in music theory. Nevertheless, when the authors are on solid ground the sentiments are admirable, right from the premiss of the book itself:

People 'play' sports and 'play' music, yet both involve hard work and discipline. Both are forms of self-expression which require a balance of spontaneity and structure, technique and inspiration. Both demand a degree of mastery over the human body, and yield immediately apparent

---

[4] This is a Pan paperback published in the UK in 1987, having appeared in 1986 from Doubleday in the USA. Its authorship is ascribed to 'Barry Green with W. Timothy Gallwey', though Gallwey is recorded as the copyright holder.

results which can give timely feedback to the performer. Since both sports and music are commonly performed in front of an audience, they also provide an opportunity for sharing the enjoyment of excellence, as well as the experience of pressure, fears and the excitement of ego involvement.

The primary discovery of the Inner Game is that, especially in our cultures of achievement-oriented activities, human beings significantly get in their own way. (p. 7)

Some people may well perform better with the help of the Green/Gallwey 'solution' to how human beings 'get in their own way', and this would be an incontestable defence of what I would otherwise dub the tennisizing of playing at music.[5] However, *The Inner Game of Music* does not seem to me to come close to some of the central impetus in where this chapter began—the anxiety of making music.

As has been indicated in various ways here, the musician is likely to be extremely sceptical about any conceptual intrusion into the activity of performance, and it is time to home in on what I regard as the real reason for this. It is epistemological, in that it concerns what musical knowledge is.

First and foremost, the danger of conceptual interference with the instinct and with the non-verbal concentration that drives skilled music-making is omnipresent. Many musicians believe that it is possible to, as it were, know too much about a piece, for instance to have such a clear and preconceived idea of the structure (formal relationships, phrase shapes, the function of pauses, ritenutos and rubatos, harmonic pace, etc.) that spontaneity of interpretation becomes impossible. There is even an ethical issue here, in the interference between conceptual thought and musical comprehension, or just simply between language and music, that arises naked and persistent in musical pedagogy. The images, often words and always *in* words, that teachers pass to

---

[5] I am told by someone who knows personally a number of world-class sportsmen as I do not (they *happen* to be men and surely women will be no different) that they are 'absolutely *fascinated* with musical performance and its exigencies'.

pupils in order to help them animate a particular passage
may remain for life, impossible to eradicate mentally (this is
when a teacher not only *demonstrates*, which is so often
how the craft of playing or singing will be handed on, but
also *articulates*, albeit poetically or in some other way that
goes outside music itself). Is it right for a teacher to fix
permanently in someone else's mind, attached to one or
another passage of music, some concept or image (rather as
Proust could never escape the unlocking of memories brought
on by the humble madeleine)? It may be singularly unhelpful
to the mature pianist to be unable to begin the development
section of the second movement of Mozart's Piano Sonata in
A minor, K. 310—four semiquavers of C major arpeggio
starting on *e* (below middle c^1), then on g^1 two quavers and
a crotchet—without hearing the words of an otherwise non-
existent song once used as a device to aid phrasing and
articulation, 'Once there was a friendly bear . . .'. Pianists
and listeners may now feel that in respect of this one melodic fragment the ethical issue is prolonged by the very
recounting of this in print (which will be excused, I hope,
since one bad case well understood may prevent many more
future ones).

Ethics aside, epistemologically we are all minded to see
the mystery of musical art as a characteristic that must be
protected against any laying bare of its essence and against
any conceptual intrusions. This is not a difficult position to
understand—though it is difficult to deal with it—since we
are entirely familiar with this form of thinking as far as it
concerns the actual composition and appreciation of music.
Since no one can actually explain why even a short passage—famously, say, the opening of Wagner's *Tristan and
Isolde*—can seem utterly entrancing to generation after generation of listeners, this kind of profound 'beauty' in the
work of art has come to be regarded as essentially inscrut-
able. It follows, in our cultural logic, that absolutely nothing
must be done to diminish that inscrutability, because this
may somehow damage our perception of that beauty or
whatever we call the experience invoked that is so highly

prized. It may even do the damage not willingly but inadvertently. *We are afraid of musical accidents*, and not irrationally but, as we shall see, perfectly reasonably. As I said before, music is always a risk.

A captivating performance of music is subject to this unyielding rule. The performer is, when all is going well (and I am not talking about a venemous rehearsal for which one has not prepared properly in any case), in the same artistic twilight as the 'inspired' composer and the 'captivated' listener. By and large, performers will say that they do not really know how they do what they do when they function, by their own lights, properly. Apart from the self-evident technical aspects, the tricks of the trade, the will to achieve the highest standards, and suitable conditions in which to work, the hidden knowledge is called 'artistry', and a fear of losing it is built into the core of Western musical life.

I will return soon to the subject of artistry and loss, which two taken together are what I would call the mysterious in performance, but meanwhile want to take a hard look at loss itself, at musical accidents. Every musician knows of pieces of music that they once loved which are now found to be empty, or sometimes even intolerable. This continual experience of loss reinforces the performer's anxious retreat from intellectual scrutiny, from theorizing. We do not really care to know why it may be that we lurch from one kind of taste to—as night follows day, and years follow years—another new focus of attention. Even worse, we also lose some music, in the sense that we do not entirely forget what we cared about, and so though the mechanism may be of no interest, the experience of saying farewell is clear. One hears of people who say they have 'lost' their technique as performers, and one can always be sure that it was something they had, or they would never lament it. Loss is real; it is not a concept that can be used approximately. No wonder performing music tends to be conducted in an atmosphere not only and sometimes not even of ecstasy, but of anxiety (from the Latin 'choke' or 'oppress'!).

There is no quick and easy solution. On the contrary, I

have been attempting to show that this is not truly an 'inner game', though its effects are played out psychologically by all players and listeners, so much as an artistic fact, part of the way that we are able to have musical knowledge in the first place. It is not something that may be eradicated or that we should ever seek to eradicate. Through understanding it better it may be that we can make use of it. At the most simple level, for instance, it is an understanding that may encourage the student and the non-professional to develop musical skills, practical skills, not only listening tastes, when it is realized that those seemingly insuperable barriers to enhanced musical achievement are only just superable to the professional too.

More profoundly, there is some purchase in the above on forming a view of what artistry means. I suppose the meaning is bound to vary from musician to musician and circumstance to circumstance, yet it is always felt to be an ineffable thing. However hard we think about artistry, we will conclude that whatever else it may be—obviously, the transcending of anxiety to start with—it is also the repository of the purely musical (or in dance, say, of pure movement). Here I join a long line of those who distinguish between conceptual and musical thought, on arguments that are barely worth rehearsing here and that have been implicit throughout this chapter.

From the performer's special point of view, however, I find it interesting that there is no escape from the complexity of deciding what one thinks artistry means, and even if the intention is not to 'solve' the question intellectually, one certainly does have to have an attitude towards it, an idea of it, a recurrent aspiration. The listener too is drawn into the inevitability of needing some grounding in this respect. It is hardly possible to attend to a performance of which one has no judgement as to quality, because it is that quality that stimulates concentration, and concentration, like loss, is not something that can be dealt with approximately.

I am sure this is as true of popular music as it is of the so-called serious repertoire, and one can certainly speak of the artistry of a Sinatra or a Jackson.[6] In 'Towards an Aesthetic of Popular Music' Simon Frith argues that popular music is somehow 'owned' by the listener in a special way.[7] Musical performance barely figures in Frith's discussion, but he ropes the subject into his sweeping and intriguing comment that 'it is not just the record that people think they own: we feel that we also possess the song itself, the particular perform-ance, and its performer' (p. 143). I think he has a much more politicized notion of artistry than I have made use of here: 'It may be', he writes, 'that, in the end, we want to value most highly that music, popular and serious, which has some sort of collective, disruptive cultural effect' (p. 149). Nevertheless his formulation, 'possessing' the particu-lar performance, reinforces my emphasis on how essential it is to have an idea of artistry. It is worth noting too that this throws up a further question once we compare live with recorded performance, because obviously there must be dif-ferent sorts of 'possession', if only in the distinction between those that can happen only once, live, and those that one may 'relive' at will through earphones, speakers, videos. This is as true for the performer as it is for the listener. Any performer will tell you that the artistry of the ephemeral is not the same as that of the permanent; and despite what I mused over earlier this distinction may after all endure in the music of the future, though we cannot discount the possibil-ity of what I called a 'fundamental shift in this situation'.

Certainly it seems that deciding how one stands in relation to artistry, be it through 'possessing' or some other mech-anism, rather trumps the academic debates about musical meaning that the reader will find in the research literature of music aesthetics and theory. In this I probably join Nicholas Cook in his conviction that discourse does not reflect how

[6] A conspicuous, thorough, slanted investigation of this mere statement is Susan McClary's *Feminine Endings: Music, Gender, and Sexuality* (Minneapolis: University of Minnesota Press, 1991), especially its final chapter.

[7] In Richard Leppert and Susan McClary (eds.), *Music and Society: The Politics of Composition, Performance and Reception* (Cambridge: Cambridge University Press, 1987), 133–49.

people *experience* music, least of all perhaps how they experience artistry. In discussing what he calls 'obscurantist thinking', Cook launches a systematic attack on forms of so-called musical 'understanding' that, implicitly or explicitly, refer to a subconscious mechanism on which such understanding depends. 'The worst thing about this sort of obscurantist thinking', he concludes,

is that it makes the listener's experience of music seem mysterious and problematical. But the experience of music is not, in itself, problematical at all; it is, in a sense, the one thing we can be sure of. The problems lie in correlating what we hear with what we think, know, or imagine.[8]

The performer's likely reaction would be to point out that this is precisely right but typically preliminary to the issues of performance studies, where the correlation of thought, knowledge, and imagination with musical experience is a constant necessity and challenge. The practising musician cannot operate, for the most part, in the atmosphere of unsullied aesthetic experience that is the supposed ideal of the ordinary, ecstatic listener—an ideal which of course I have been questioning in any case. The apparent problems are at the centre of the activity. Cook, as an author, has no choice but to formulate an answer to them that will stand forever in the library. The performer has to address them time and again.

The intention has certainly not been to increase anxiety or give any sort of last word on artistry. It is best, or so I would claim, to recognize what goes on—to ask, rather than deny it, why music is threatened by words; to admit that musicians are afraid of accidents (conceptual ones, and musical parapraxes) and are not in a perpetual psychic bliss; to confront the fact that artistry is not served on a plate free.

[8] *Music, Imagination, and Culture,* 230.

4

Recent Thought

I think that the ideal way to go about making a performance . . . is to assume that when you begin, you don't quite
know what it is about. You only come to know as you
proceed.

(Glenn Gould, *The Glenn Gould Reader*)

Chapters 2 and 3 have outlined the challenges, both 'dis-
ciplinary' and mental and artistic, awaiting those who are
interested in investigating performance studies—in its very
general sense pertaining as much to the listener as to the
practitioner. I have had to present so far an account largely
of what is 'missing'; we can now turn for most of the rest
of this volume to what is present. If I have had to insist so
far on problematics, as an antidote to the customary starting-
point in one or another related text, which so often strikes
me as a complacent starting-point, this doesn't mean that we
should ignore much that is positive and purposeful in the
existing literature, and in the debates that are in the air
currently. Some of this will now be addressed.

The comparison between sport and music was instructive
but perhaps dispiriting, or at least challenging, for the aims
and methods, motivations and vicissitudes of sport seem so
clear in comparison with those of music. With relief we can
look at another comparison, with the theatre actor. It is
almost uplifting to contemplate what the performer of music
has available compared with the bereft actor. Covering an
immense repertoire of music, for example, are the scales and
arpeggios of common-practice tonality, absorbed by all players
and singers of classical music during their training. A command of scales and arpeggios, though it has been argued

against unrealistically in my opinion by such as Matthay decades ago and Kolisch recently, is not merely a physical resource, but a mental ordering of sound that arms us to understand and be able to control actual music. There is some analogy here with, for instance, the handbooks on body gesture that were compulsory study for European actors in the late eighteenth century, and certainly one might also point to the affinity between the place of the large critical literature on Shakespeare, and the large critico-analytical literature on Beethoven's music, in the preparation of the performer for theatre stage or concert-hall and opera-house.

Effectively, however, Western acting is simply not susceptible to the coherence and extent of theorizing that has been characteristic of musical culture in recent centuries—from the Guidonian hand found in treatises of the late thirteenth century, a mnemonic for the hexachordal system partitioning the nearly three-octave scale then covered by various registers of the human voice; to the latest guides to computer-aided instruction in so-called Aural Training. The musician's wealth of practical training material is what provides that fluid 'motor' ability to pass through musical time in performance without giving conscious thought to the multiple, vastly complex effort involved: it teaches the musician to 'walk', 'run', 'jump', indeed we might even say to 'speak music'. None of the mighty influx of trainings is apparent to the audience, but it is important to know that this is what performer and audience have in common. It does not divide, it unites, for it is no more apparent to the highly skilled than it is to the casual observer.

When it does become apparent, this must mean that there has been some form of error (the horn 'cracks' a note, the singer goes flat, the conductor completely misjudges a tempo —what a list one could make of what can go wrong!), and admittedly the skilled musician is then likely to spot precisely what the trouble has been in a way that cannot be expected of an 'ordinary listener'. If the skilled performer takes some pleasure in knowing what is going on when trouble arises, it is surely not through conceit, through the enjoyment of superiority, but merely a professional logging—'there but for the grace of God go I, and I'm glad I heard and learned from it, though I'd rather all had gone well'.

Not only does the performer have a rich tradition of technical training on which to draw, underpinning that precious artistry which figured in Chapter 3, but in the contemporary musical climate an almost overwhelming knowledge of many different sorts has become necessary. Like it or not, there cannot now be an innocent performer, if ever there could. Although it would have been a distraction to bring this in to my earlier argument about the epistemological tension between music and concept, I would add here that this is yet another factor that ratchets up the difficulties, that justifies placing anxiety firmly on the map early on.

Thurston Dart discussed the essential new knowledge in respect of the performance of 'early music':

The problem . . . has only arisen during the last century and a half, for until the early years of the nineteenth century no musician was interested in anything but new music, that is to say, music written during the preceding forty or fifty years. . . . The important thing for us to realise is that a tremendous change has taken place, and that as a result the composer of the present day has to compete for his living with men long dead—many of them unquestioned masters of music in their own time as well as in ours, but others who were once thought of as fine extemporisers and little more. We are imprisoned by the past. The whole upbringing of a modern musician, whether he is a composer, a performer or a listener, is based on playing, hearing reading and analysing old music. . . . The modern musician's approach to the music of his own time is obstructed by the past, and his approach to old music is through the gateway of the present.[1]

[1] Thurston Dart, *The Interpretation of Music* (4th edn., London: Hutchinson, 1967), 160–1. To the modern reader aware of literary-critical trends in the 1970s and 1980s Dart's words will have an eerily prophetic ring of Harold Bloom's poetic theory, first disseminated in *The Anxiety of Influence* (Oxford: Oxford University Press, 1973). Recently Bloom's ideas about creativity in relation to cultural legacy have become fashionable among a number of music historians. See, for an example of a major study influenced partly by Bloom that has stirred up controversy in the musicological journals, Joseph N. Straus's *Remaking the Past: Musical Modernism and the Influence of the Tonal Tradition* (Cambridge, Mass.: Harvard University Press, 1990).

There is now even more 'obstruction' of a kind he did not live to witness, the 'gateway' now also involving the microchip and all that has followed from it musically, and the panculturalism of art in the late twentieth century. Nevertheless Dart is, as it happens, still right in asserting that we are 'imprisoned by the past'. In the decades since he wrote, it could easily have been that people would have begun to lose interest in 'old' music, but in fact that interest seems to have grown beyond any degree that might have been predicted.

Dart writes of the composer, performer, and listener, but I would hesitate to allow that the burden of historical responsibility is spread equally across all those engaged with music. Just as, to return to my image in Chapter 1, the listener will, whether through wearing earplugs or who knows what other form of unintended control, render all performance contingent, so the performer renders composition contingent. There is a chain of dependency here with the performer as the crucial link. C. P. E. Bach wrote in 1753 about the pivotal authority of the performer:

What comprises good performance? The ability through singing or playing to make the ear conscious of the true content and affect of a composition. Any passage can be so radically changed by modifying its performance that it will be barely recognizable.[2]

I have cited sources from the mid-eighteenth and twentieth centuries under the heading 'Recent Thought' not mischievously but to signal the fact that we are not here involved in the invention of some serious problem which we can then fail to solve (as Hans Keller would have put it). I am deliberately not going to offer a history of performance studies but want to indicate here and there that what we are concerned with is an important topic that has occupied minds

[2] *Essay on the True Art of Playing Keyboard Instruments*, trans. and ed. William J. Mitchell (London: Eulenberg, 1974), 148. The *Essay*, Part 1 of which was first published in 1753, counts among the most important documents ever penned about musical performance as a repository of 18th-c. practice and wisdom.

going back very many generations. It is the centre of it, for our purposes, in the late twentieth century, that has to be found.

A pioneering step was taken with the publication of Erwin Stein's *Form and Performance*.[3] Stein had the vision to realize that general points could be made about performance factors—his observations about the essential difference between the articulation of repeated pitches compared with that of conjunct and disjunct intervals, to take one case, is widely applicable, an illuminating insight:

> If notes are merely repeated, it goes without saying that the rhythm is more significant than the 'line'. Unfortunately it is a bad habit of string players and clarinettists not sufficiently to articulate, but to blur, the rhythm of repeated notes, especially if they are within a passage of *legato* character. (pp. 29–30)

He was also specific, illustrating from mostly 'old' music, as Dart would have called it, yet with the credibility that derives from his obvious engagement with issues of contemporaneous musical life, as a musician who was not only 'imprisoned by the past' but also evidently nourished by it.

It is worth quoting from his Preface passages which reveal the issues that he believed to be at stake:

> I do not underrate the examples of great performers. Gifted students can learn a great deal from them, but they sometimes accept their vices together with their virtues. *The details of performance have never systematically been investigated* [Stein's emphasis]. Nor do the customary analyses help the performer . . . We find in the text of the music only more or less vague indications—if any. The intelligent musician is supposed to feel instinctively at what rate, and how loud or soft, the notes are meant to follow each other. But the intelligent musician often goes wrong. A sense of proportion is often lacking, especially as regards music's extension in time . . . The average listener enjoys music's physical sensation. The performer is tempted to supply in abundance what is most in demand . . . But worse, it is the performers themselves who, with rare exceptions, vaguely feel rather than precisely understand the

[3] With 'Foreword' by Benjamin Britten (London: Faber and Faber, 1962).

relations of the notes. If they knew, they would not tolerate the wrong accents that occur in almost every phrase ... Melody, harmony, texture, rhythm, dynamics and colour are the elements of musical form and, though they are inseparable and interdependent, in performance each of the elements as well as their mutual relations must be taken into account. For performance is a function of musical form. (pp. 12–14)

Obviously Stein was a 'formalist', offering solutions rather than outlining difficulties, as is borne out throughout his remarkable book. Yet consider what he puts on the table in the narrative I have abstracted above: first, you mustn't trust what great performers pass on; second, 'the details of performance have never systematically been investigated' (I can find no synopsis of that curt and pregnant statement); third, music analysis in the 1950s and before did not help (see Chapter 7, as also concerning points four, six, and seven following); fourth, composers' notation does not tell us how to do things in real musical time; fifth, listeners normally seek a physical thrill and the performer will in the main provide it; sixth, performers don't usually understand what they are doing because they don't examine the part in relation to the whole; seventh, the structure of the music tells you how to perform it. Is any professional to be found who would disagree with this seven-point agenda? There will always be emphasis, for each practitioner has individual methods, and I for one am much keener on points two, four, and six than the other four. Still, the only things wrong from our perspective with *Form and Performance* are that only a trained musician can understand it, which is hardly a fault given its intended audience, and that it is of its structuralist time when it was possible to propose, ascetically, that 'performance is a function of musical form'.

There is a 'hands on' feel to *Form and Performance* that is regrettably lacking in more recent books by Cone[4] and Berry[5] which may come to the performer's attention, though

[4] Edward T. Cone, *Musical Form and Musical Performance* (New York: Norton, 1968), supplemented by 'Musical Form and Musical Performance Reconsidered', *Music Theory Spectrum*, 7 (1985), 149–58.
[5] Wallace Berry, *Musical Structure and Performance* (New Haven, Conn.: Yale University Press, 1989).

neither of these latter writers was dealing with the practical matters of performance, and both were trying to hook their readers' interest on to aesthetic and theoretical ideologies. I mention them in passing because they exemplify, a couple of decades on from Stein and also just a few years ago the persistence of structuralist approaches to 'academic' studies of musical performance, approaches that seek information about the musical work *within* the work itself. And along with this has progressed the sceptical response of those engaged in performance research, for instance the American scholar John Rink, who summarizes his pragmatic, dubious view of Berry's tough analytical stance in the following words:

Perhaps a little less rigour and a little more subjective, 'generalized reflection' (possibly on the basis of 'informed intuition') might have inspired those penetrating insights into the music—not just the music's structure—that are essential to truly enlightened performance.[6]

If the 'centre' is not necessarily to be found in structuralist approaches, I nevertheless insist (and will in due course attempt to demonstrate practically) that what the musical performer has available, beyond 'trainings', is decisively more useful in the technical than in the impressionistic sphere (the sphere of 'informed intuition'). The impressionistic sphere ripples with memoirs, guides, handbooks. I am not going to list examples of impressionistic writing on performance that belong on the coffee table, if they can be said to belong anywhere at all. Stein's dignified dismissal of this literature—'I do not underrate the examples of great performers'—is an estimable attitude. For the curious, however, I note one recent extreme example offered by one of the world's leading publishing houses, Fernando Valenti's *A Performer's Guide to the Keyboard Partitas of J. S. Bach*.[7] It is, like a newspaper article, one person's view, devoid of cultural support, as if two centuries of painstaking research can count for nothing, including directly relevant case-studies, for instance, in Hermann

[6] Review of Berry (see above, n. 5) in *Music Analysis*, 9/3 (Oct. 1990), 319–39 (p. 338).
[7] (New Haven, Conn.: Yale University Press, 1989).

Keller's *Phrasing and Articulation*.[8] As a body of work, it merits mention only for cautionary purposes, to make it clear that this is certainly not what Gould meant by writing that 'you only come to know as you proceed'. Gould was discussing (with Artur Rubinstein) what it *feels* like to walk into the recording studio. He of all twentieth-century performers would argue that there is no end to the thirst for musical knowledge that informs the performer's preparation, and an unscholarly, haphazard approach at that stage will have a direct effect in degrading the music that is eventually made.

Almost at the beginning of this enquiry it was pointed out that 'musicians think hard', and already from this brief survey it is apparent that there are complex issues to contend with. What the musical performer has available beyond what I called trainings drives us into all the nooks and crannies of contemporary intellectual life, from 'tennisizing' to structuralism, from relativism (and that is what Chapter 1's ear-plugs were about) to the postmodern craze for a literary approach to musical understanding.[9] Once again I am moving towards a call for orientation, and I think this will be achieved when we recognize the inevitability of the coexistence of music and discourse, and not shy away from it into the retreats of fragmentary subdisciplines, with mute performers, and arid commentators.

This underlying image of fragmentation is not of my making and is endemic in a proportion—maybe even the majority—of those who take it upon themselves to put forward their

[8] (London: Barrie and Rockliff, 1966).
[9] I do not use the word 'craze' in an offhand way. There is a mania currently among book and journal editors for material of this kind, and I have written elsewhere in the specialist literature about the phenomenon. A summary of what I have said would be roughly: 'Do we actually need to approach music through literary and quasi-philosophical theories that may not be as good, as *strong*, as existing musical theories?' Of the many literary-musical publications I have seen in recent years perhaps the outstanding volume is Steven Paul Scher (ed.), *Music and Text: Critical Inquiries* (Cambridge: Cambridge University Press, 1992). Something like a sixth of Scher's multi-authored book is taken up in various ways with matters of performance studies, but in an interdisciplinary spirit that excludes it from being of use here.

understanding of the musical world. It has been widely disseminated in particular by Joseph Kerman, a glittering writer
on music whose words deserve to be weighed scrupulously.
It must give great pause for thought that Kerman is so convinced of the ineffability of music-making and music appreciation. He presents himself as completely unable to find 'gift'
or 'artistry' (my words) in the way performance is observed,
or the way arguments about it are conducted. This leaning
comes nevertheless from an author who is committed to the
orientation of musical studies towards humanistic criticism
and away from formalist structuralism. Presumably, humanistic criticism is, at its best, truly 'gifted' criticism, something
that is done well. Kerman tells us, though, that performers
are 'the doers, not the talkers', with every right to an intellectual detachment that may 'range anywhere from mild
dilettantish curiosity to outright derision', and his best accolade of the literature surrounding their art is that some of it
can be 'thoughtful':

Reading the best of these books, written by some who are among the
most distinguished in their fields and also among the most thoughtful,
one finds the authors returning again and again to the problem of
interpretation, as I have tried to formulate it: the way in which the
musician's individuality is to be brought to bear on the individuality
of works of art.[10]

To the extent that Kerman is outlining a much more sophisticated critique with his sniffy word 'talkers' than I did
above with my sniffy term 'coffee table', I cannot take issue,
and the publication of his *Musicology* brought a welcome
debunking of all sorts of musicological myths. Still, it seems
to me hardly possible to square his abolutist position with
the actual role that has been played by discourse in performance over the centuries in the development of musical practice,
from C. P. E. Bach's *Essay*, through, for example, some of
Schumann's critical writings, to such a monumental work as
Heinrich Schenker's book on Beethoven's Ninth Symphony,[11]

[10] *Musicology* (London: Fontana Paperbacks, 1985), 196.
[11] *Beethovens neunte Sinfonie* (Vienna: Universal Edition, 1912).

which was studied by very many conductors and players in pre-Second World War Vienna and beyond. In C. P. E. Bach we find a compendium of practical knowledge and theory: in Schumann, besides much else, an attempt to explain the paths new music was taking, to understand the stylistics of different national traditions, to assess what features could be identified as of high quality in Romantic musical performance; in Schenker, an explanation of the deep and sustained musical coherence of a seminal masterpiece, coherence that may be shattered in detail and overall in any shoddy interpretation.

It seems rather that at each point in the progress of (modern) music history there has been a deep concern to explicate the cultural constraints upon musical interpretation, to assess the performer's involvement with a style, which is not only an individual matter. This has been argued out many times in recent musical scholarship, with all the inflections that represent different musicological and music-theoretical interest groups. When style is explained through a complex, indeed complicated form of abstract theorizing, as one undoubtedly finds in the abstruse Schenker, the average musician will feel out of touch with the issues at stake, quite understandably; and this is what Kerman means, in part, by 'the talkers', taking the opportunity time and again in *Musicology* to complain about them. However, in trying to assess the significance of different forms of thinking for issues of performance, above all the issues of 'interpretation' in its broadest sense, it is not enough to resort to such a polarized question as the following, which is the sort of question of which I guess Kerman would approve: 'what does this mean purely to the individual artist confronted purely by the artistic essence of a certain piece of music?' As Roger Sessions observes laconically, 'one must . . . accustom oneself to the fact that the performance of music is not an entirely simple affair'.[12] There are, that is, no pure 'doers', as I hope to have shown in this chapter from a fourth angle.

---

[12] Cf. above, Ch. 2 n. 8.

5

The Romantic Legacy

Obviously, it is not without a reason that the worst inter-
preters usually tackle the Romantics.

(Igor Stravinsky, *Poetics of Music*)

In my experience of taking bright students through their
music analysis classes, dissecting the forms, textures, rhythms,
tonalities, notations, texts—whatever there *is* to try to understand in the works of fine composers—I have been confronted
countless times by one question: 'Did the composer know
about this?' It takes a long time to put all the facts in a
particular case that may persuade the student both that the
composer did not know and, however, that this is not relevant, that what matters is what we ourselves know. Long
ago I put this pedagogical problem to a lively American
colleague noted for her ability to spread knowledge and
enlightenment among her charges: 'Just tell them "Sure! The
composer knew!"' she said, 'then change the subject'.

Musicians are inherently curious about their 'authors' and
artistically loyal to them. Their 'authors', on the other hand,
have become in approximately the last two centuries reticent
about explaining what they think goes into the act of musical
composition. At least, this turn of events is what is in the
popular mind. I often wish that Beethoven had taken a little
time out to write, as I'm sure he could easily have done, a
handy textbook for composers or at least a longish letter
saying 'what it is really like doing what I do', along with a
few of his notoriously reticent heirs—Brahms of course, then
Debussy, and Birtwistle to this day.

The image of the deaf *and silent* genius has created an
unhelpful mythology that has long outlived its nineteenth-

century origins. We would do much better to marvel at the rich aura of verbal articulacy, of self-awareness, that encompasses Romantic and post-Romantic composition: Schumann (as already mentioned), Berlioz, Wagner, Schoenberg, Stravinsky, Boulez . . . it is another of those impossibly extensive lists with which we are bound to be confronted in this kind of work.

I intend these points to lay out a sense of the grip of Romantic ideology in our post-Romantic times. Players and listeners alike are caught up in this swirling scenario whether they recognize it or not. As Arnold Whittall observes, 'The Romantic period, age or era grew out of, and vigorously away from, Classicism; and so powerful was that growth that when the twentieth century is too far in the past to be described as 'Modern', it may well be called the post-Romantic age'.[1]

There are of course those who would argue that we are still in a stage of Romanticism, however late a stage it may be, and it has also been observed in many sources that the 'romantic' is present in every cultural 'period', of which ours can be no exception. Just what is the measure of the conflict between Romantic and Modern is going to vary, greatly perhaps, depending on where it manifests itself. For instance, from a purely technical point of view the musical executant is not going to notice a significant difference in difficulty between difficult compositions of 1840 and 1940. Although in the twentieth century there have been many new techniques (new ways that instruments are played, new instruments, new aural, that is, pitch challenges to the human voice), I would maintain that the virtuosity of some early Romantic music, in its purely physical demands, is more or less at the limits of possible human achievement and is never going to be significantly exceeded. When it comes to the 'language' of music, however, the conflict between new and old has been, as everybody knows, radical to a degree that has divided culture and, as has often been discussed, alienated many a composer from many an audience, and from many

---

[1] *Romantic Music* (London: Thames and Hudson, 1987), 12.

a performer. The 'paths of modern music', as Paul Griffiths summarizes them in *A Concise History of Modern Music*, cleave modern music from its Romantic antecedents: 'the abandonment of traditional tonality, the development of new rhythmic complexity, the recognition of colour as an essential, the creation of a quite new form for each work, the exploration of deeper mental processes'.[2]

If I thus admit the relationship between Romantic and Modern to be labile, it is nevertheless a psychological factor whether active or dormant. So omnipresent is it in modern musical culture that Eugene Narmour, an authority on the psychology of music, ascribes to it a complete shift in the work of performance studies:

Traditionally performers have envisioned their obligations almost wholly in terms of their responsibilities to the composer—doubtless a holdover of nineteenth-century Romantic beliefs about composers being both priests and prophets, the saints of culture leading their supplicants (performers and listeners alike) to ever-new realms of self-awareness. But this is myopic. For as cognitive psychology has taught us, the temporal materialization of a musical artwork emanates not from the composer alone or from the performer alone but from a triarchical interrelationship among composer, performer *and* listener. The composer produces a score, a kind of syntactical roadmap based on a highly efficient but therefore limited symbol system whose interpretation even in the relatively highly specified notation of Western culture is indisputably still partly dependent on oral tradition. The performer attempts to bring that score to life, in the process modifying it to fit with his or her own aesthetic beliefs, stylistic experiences, and tradition of learning. And listeners complete the interpretation by *actively* bringing to bear their own peculiar cognitive expectations based on their own idiosyncratic learning of the style.[3]

I have already offered my own brief account of the 'triarchical interrelationship' (see above, p. 42), but note how Narmour

[2] (London: Thames and Hudson, 1978), 13. Music historians are deeply suspicious of such generalizations, but few would deny that Griffiths puts his finger on some essentials here.
[3] 'On the Relationship of Analytical Theory to Performance and Interpretation', in Eugene Narmour and Ruth A. Solie (eds.), *Explorations in Music, the Arts, and Ideas* (Stuyvesant, NY: Pendragon Press, 1988), 317–40 (p. 318).

characterizes it—he's in no doubt—as a supplanting of 'Romantic beliefs'. Note how *contemptuous* he is about those 'beliefs'. Is it right to wipe away the ethos of the music many performers and listeners still like best? Is it even possible? I have been arguing here that some of the 'authentic' ethos will always remain or at the least promise (Narmour would doubtless say threaten) to reappear.

One way to try to understand this better is to expose the simple facts of the situation, and in this I return to my own notion—which is designed to be anything but contemptuous—of the Ecstasy school (Chapter 3). It is simply the case that musicians active and passive, and be it 'myopic' or not, actually cherish the resonances of Romanticism with which they grew up. All children (those who are blessed with food and warmth) believe in some kind of magic, and surely this experience never entirely leaves us. The idea that some nights Chopin just dipped his pen in moonlight and composed Nocturnes, he knew not how, is an idea we *like*. We do not particularly want to give it up in some harsh, modernist cause. We believe that art contains the breath of life itself, it is *inspired*.

There are any number of ways in which this translates into hard-nosed musical reality. Tempo, for example, has been much written about in this respect. Arnold Schoenberg, one of the founding fathers of musical modernism, wrote that it is completely misconceived to suppress the variable metrical characteristics of nineteenth-century music and music subsequently written in its spirit. It is especially piquant to read these views of a man who was vilified all his life for his supposed overturning of musical convention. The passage is taken from Schoenberg's article of 1948 entitled 'Today's Manner of Performing Classical Music':

Today's manner of performing classical music of the so-called 'romantic' type, suppressing all emotional qualities and all unnotated changes of tempo and expression, derives from the style of playing primitive dance music. This style came to Europe by way of America, where no old culture regulated presentation, but where a certain frigidity of feeling reduced all musical expression. Thus almost everywhere in

Europe music is played in a stiff, inflexible metre—not in a tempo, i.e. according to a yardstick of freely measured quantities. Astonishingly enough, almost all European conductors and instrumentalists bowed to this dictate without resistance. All were suddenly afraid to be called romantic, ashamed of being called sentimental. . . . Why is music written at all? Is it not a romantic feeling which makes you listen to it? Why do you play the piano when you could show the same skill on a typewriter?[4]

Schoenberg was not alone in his strong reaction against what has been called 'monometric' rhythm. There was a feeling that in the monometric style promulgated above all by Stravinsky, which might be appropriate for his own compositions, there was a net loss in the performance of Classical and Romantic music. Recently, Richard Taruskin has argued persuasively that modern 'authenticist' approaches to rhythmic performance practice in earlier repertories are equally misconceived. Far from being historically informed, they merely reflect the modern, anti-Romantic Stravinskian attitude. Taruskin is certainly not attacking Stravinsky as a composer, but assessing his historical place in musical performance. 'Stravinsky's own performance', he notes of a Mozart recording, 'is execution, pure and simple. You could not hope to find a drier, harder—in a word, more geometrical—performance of any music. You cannot say that the man did not practise what he preached' (p. 183).[5]

My actual presentation of the Romantic legacy thus far has been necessarily broad, and there is always the danger of peddling vagary. To counteract this, what follows is a case-study of some genuine Romantic material. It is of the highest quality, selected not only for that, but also because it exemplifies, almost dramatizes, the aesthetic chasm between the sort of post-Romantic, formalist thinking we saw in Stein (beginning with the familiar), and what might be called a contemporaneous, Romantic 'performance studies environment'. The subject is playing Beethoven, who was

[4] *Style and Idea* (London: Faber and Faber, 1975), 320–1.
[5] 'The Pastness of the Present', in Nicholas Kenyon (ed.), *Authenticity and Early Music* (Oxford: Oxford University Press, 1988), 137–207.

alive (43) and composing at the time of this essay of 1813. It is by the poet and composer E. T. A. Hoffmann:

Now, as regards difficulty, the correct and fitting performance of a work of Beethoven's asks nothing more than that one should understand him, that one should enter deeply into his being, that—conscious of one's own consecration—one should boldly dare to step into the circle of the magical phenomena that his powerful spell has evoked. He who is not conscious of this consecration, who regards sacred Music as a mere game, as a mere entertainment for an idle hour, as a momentary stimulus for dull ears, or as a means of self-ostentation— let him leave Beethoven's music alone.... The true artist lives only in the work that he has understood as the composer meant it and that he then performs. He is above putting his own personality forward in any way, and all his endeavors are directed toward a single end—that all the wonderful enchanting pictures and apparitions that the composer has sealed into his work with magic power may be called into active life, shining in a thousand colors, and that they may surround mankind in luminous sparkling circles and, enkindling its imagination, its innermost soul, may bear it in rapid flight into the faraway spirit realm of sound.[6]

It's enough to make Professor Narmour's blood boil. Yet it is also profoundly authentic in that, as countless nineteenth-century writers testify, Hoffmann caught the spirit of the age. His words were studied carefully. They not only were part of early nineteenth-century musical (and literary) thought, but they shaped it, they became its assumptions.

What we have to do to play Beethoven, Hoffmann dictates, in the pre-Nietzschean age, is become Beethoven, understand him musically in the way that he understood himself, and be replaced by the composer—ecstatic, transported. Hoffmann is not suggesting that this happens with a snap of the fingers, like an instantly conjured magic spell. Far from it: what he is discussing is the difficulty of doing what is 'correct' and

---

[6] Oliver Strunk, *Source Readings in Music History* (New York: Norton, 1950), 780–1. The quotation is from Hoffmann's essay 'Beethoven's Instrumental Music', and is cited here from the first edition of Strunk, among various possible sources, because this is by far the most widely available in libraries around the world.

'fitting'. It is something one must 'dare' to do, and do it 'boldly'. Hoffmann allows that music may be an 'entertainment' or a 'momentary stimulus', and a way of showing off—concepts with which I cannot imagine any reader having a problem in identifying. But that is not what Beethoven is so to speak 'about', nor is it the proper work of the 'true artist'. We also have to be complete, fully integrated personalities, all endeavours 'directed toward a single end'. That is how to fly to the faraway spirit realm of sound. A tall order.

Those unfamiliar with authentic Romantic sentiments may feel overwhelmed and it is worth bearing in mind that Romantic idealism is just that, a position without compromise, not intended to be a reasonable attitude. Nor is it supposed to offer a challenge to the conscious mind, and it is this conscious reasoning—how do I *make* this happen?—that Hoffmann stops in its tracks. In his classic text, *The Mind of the European Romantics*, H. G. Schenk captured this difference of attitude in an excellent formulation that I think does really help us to feel we can understand it:

In our century, it was stated by Igor Stravinsky that music is the only sphere in which man consciously experiences the present. The remark is typical for the approach of the rationalist: no Romantic would have made it. For the Romantics, who in general preferred to live as it were in the past or the future, music constituted the sphere in which the present could best be experienced in a kind of enchanting dream.[7]

There is ample evidence to show that the 'doers' and 'talkers' of the time thought in terms of entirely different criteria, 'Romantic' ones, that as I have been trying to show may be hard now for us to comprehend. Kerman rightly links the criteria of Romantic aesthetics to the early ideology of modern theory.[8] Yet it is equally important to accept this aesthetic approach on its own terms, not because of some hollow welcome for yet another dose of authenticity, but in order to emphasize that there was a time when artists and their

[7] (London: Constable, 1966), 232.
[8] *Musicology* (London: Fontana Paperbacks, 1985), 64–7.

audiences really did think in the ways that we now find perhaps incomprehensible and at least a little embarrassing. Though I have said earlier that the Romantic may still be with us or indeed present in any period, we cannot deny the sense of historical distance when taking a serious look at the early nineteenth century and perhaps much that came after. Certainly there is nothing pragmatic in what Hoffmann demands. To take him at his word would—ironically, given our tendency towards an ecstatic assimilation of music— seem to be a much more difficult step than to be a wholesale exponent of musical formalism. Most people, I suppose, can form a decent impression of what it might feel like to take a stringently formalist, calculating approach to musical performance (and, presumably, 'outright derision' could be justified only from someone who had been able to gain this impression). There are many among the modern performance community, however, who could not even begin to subscribe seriously to the kind of artistic creed that drove, not only Hoffmann, but successive generations of Romantic music-makers.

I think it follows that the problems of discussing musical performance productively are not as they are often characterized. They vary in any case between communities, as is obvious in the British tendency to worship intuition, the French love of epistemology, or the American ideal of discursive clarity. But a common thread is that modern society is not given to the sort of clarity of purpose that we suppose was the case in earlier ages, and any sectional argument about artistic activity must incorporate this aspect of the present human condition, of the 'uneasy state of mind' to which I have already referred.

We do not have to go very far back in the history of music to arrive at realms firmly beyond our grasp, far less retrievable than the Romantic legacy. The organization of music according to rhetorical principles in Bach, for instance (that is, his ordering of musical proportions and 'affects' in a way that corresponds to Graeco-Roman principles of good oratory), which is certainly reflected not solely in his compositional processes, but significantly in his performance practice, is beyond the modern experience, and we know it: we're aware of a potential clarity that remains veiled. The music aesthetician could argue, and one day a neurologist might well show, that it is precisely the reflection of this clarity in the musical composition that draws us to it and provides, through our artistic experience, a vision to which we cannot gain access conceptually and, perhaps, emotionally— that is, regardless of whether 'we know it' or not. While that may be true, it does not remove the conceptual awareness of, and, I would posit, normal acceptance of, a historical barrier, and conceptual awareness of this kind of intellectual defeat shapes the work that a performer does, not necessarily on stage, but in the lifelong development of skills and attitudes.

The deep-seated idealism of the early nineteenth century no longer exists either, for all the continuities which, as I have indicated, do persist. Hoffmann illustrates another, more recent historical barrier. In this case, though, the insulation is by no means complete. Romantic idealism still has its resonances—after all, it seems highly unlikely that any reader would completely fail to grasp anything of Hoffmann's meaning in the quotation above. What performer, if only as an avid listener, has not experienced that kind of noumenal moment, in the apperception of some music by Beethoven, that Hoffmann describes as a 'necessary and ongoing condition'? The problem is that our engagement is in the main, as the authentic Romantic might say, half-*hearted* (or at least fractionally-hearted, as I would say in the inevitable mixed metaphor of the pre-twenty-first century).

If this is tantamount to declaring how much easier life would be, if only performers felt much, much *more* distant from the Romantic repertoire, it might seem itself a heroic overstatement. The delicacy of what is at stake can be measured by assessing the repertoire. The performer who decides that the imponderables of semi- or pseudo-Romanticism can no longer be coped with may pay the terrible price of isolation (in fact, unemployment). This kind of stinging reality certainly does happen. I know of one eminent clarinet soloist who no longer dares play Mozart, let alone record Mozart, because he knows how to do it only in the post-Romantic manner of his training, and this is politically incorrect, unacceptable to the authenticist 'authorities' in the music business.

The easier life is a phantom in any case because our experience of the Romantic is never fully formed. In the 1960s, the listener's grasp of the Romantic symphony, and expectations in hearing Romantic symphonies for the first time, and the performer's attitude to it, would have been shaped by a knowledge of a repertory that is still in play—Beethoven, Schumann, Brahms, Tchaikovsky. It's another impossible list. Not on that list, though, would have been Mahler, whom the musical world in general had not at the time 'discovered'. Only in 1960 was a collected edition of Mahler's compositions begun, and the record catalogues and concert programmes of the time are virtually bare of his name. Considering the phenomenal impact that the fashion for Mahler's music has made everywhere in the last two or three decades (I use the word 'fashion', if it can be said to have a best possible sense, in its best possible sense), it must be that our very image of Romanticism has changed, filtered as it now is through our assimilation of this particular late 'flowering', as it has often been described. Beethoven—this is one way of putting it—will never seem the same again. Another contingency (cf. Chapter 1), another imponderable for the performer.

We are continually confronted with the idealism of Romantic and a great deal of post-Romantic art and thinking. It is best to know of this, to keep it constantly in mind as performers and, as we all also are, as audience. Nietzsche, who was in the thick of it, portrayed Romanticism as a form of 'fatality', in the decades after Hoffmann when 'a kind of enchanting dream' (see Schenk above) lost its philosophical innocence. It is certainly a force to be reckoned with from— as a true Romantic would have it—that first little-fingered one-octave C major scale to that last old-age musing on what music, and everything else, meant.

6

The Sound of Music

Musicians wrestle everywhere—
All day—among the crowded air
I hear the silver strife—

(Emily Dickinson)

Clearly, I am going to try to do something more here than reassert that the hills are alive with it—though the sound of music be impossible to convey in words. I stick to my insistence that music makes us think in performance or as performers, and it is certainly no less the sound than other of its aspects that stimulates our pondering, speculation, desire to understand. Studies of this particular aspect, apart from the ecstatic ones, naturally tend to veer either towards the minutiae of acoustics, which for the specialist is an endlessly fascinating subject, or towards the psychology of perception.[1] These poles will always be within sight in what follows in this chapter, but viewed from the middle path of practical considerations.

Practically speaking, there is a vast horizon of different points of attention to the sound of music. For the listener this may arise in all sorts of ways. I have already, for instance, raised the unanswered question about the relative value of different forms of sound reproduction (see above, Ch. 1)—note that it is unanswered rather than unanswerable, for surely the day will come when the physical processes of sound production and of sound reception in the ear will have been described sufficiently congruently for it to be clear

---

[1] This is anything but a new musical sub-discipline, but it did leap into prominence in the 1980s, for instance through the launch in 1983 of a quarterly research journal, *Music Perception* (University of California Press).

what kind of reproduction (in what acoustic environment) most resembles real perceived sound. With an eye to the other pole, I have also raised a psychological question of attention by pointing out that, if you notice it or decide to listen out for it, the highest register of a piano can sometimes sound more like Schoenberg's typewriter than do the lower registers of the instrument. The general question of attention is mundane anyway: we all know what it's like when suddenly our brain can no longer filter out the low-level noise of the person in the next seat at the concert-hall or opera-house who has a sub-clinical but audible nasal constriction—that is, our attention shifts *suddenly*, and thus through no fault of the neighbour nose we hear low-level noise masking the music. All the time the listener is faced with questions of sound, not surprisingly of the very medium of music.

To the performer this is no less true, but perhaps in a sense it is also 'more' true, for every performer has sonic challenges. I suppose the most often discussed, the highest common factor, is when you can't properly hear what you are doing. Our 'proverbial second violinist' (see Introduction) who 'gave up music years ago' will have been turned off in part because hard work yields nothing: you concentrate so hard that you can't sit back and listen while playing to the oddly balanced sound heard in the middle of an orchestra, but nor is there any feedback from your own efforts because the vibrations from the violin inches from the ear are entirely swamped by those from the rest of the orchestra in the adjacent thousand-or-so square metres. Singers in choral societies the world over (indeed, in tribal incantations) do not seem to have this difficulty, doubtless because the vibrations of one's own voice come to the brain through a different route.[2] 'Not hearing' may also be an acoustic problem quite separate from anything the players are doing. Some practice rooms with their heavy sound-proofing are almost

---

[2] This kind of different route is considered in (expert) passing by Oliver Sacks in *Seeing Voices* (Berkeley, Calif.: University of California Press, 1990), 8 n. 14.

anechoic and the lack of reverberation may disorient perception significantly. Some large halls seem to suck the sound off the stage leaving the player or singer feeling acoustically detached, a strange experience of being remote from the physically adjacent. Professionals report this of some of our favourite auditoria in Berlin, Birmingham, London, New York, Vienna . . . !

The lowest common denominator is the different sonic challenge of each activity. Compare for instance the string player with the pianist. The violinist has to develop a left/right arm-and-hand difference of great complexity. The left hand uses myriads of finger movements, while the right-hand fingers have just one job to do in supporting and guiding the bow (not that this is a simple matter, but the fingers work together to one purpose). The left and right arms have to work, not in opposite planes, but at about a ninety-degree angle to each other.[3] The pianist, in contrast, works on making symmetrical opposites move fluently and similarly, so that—to put it in one easily understood way—no listener should be able to tell which hand is playing, to tell from the sound whether the thumb is on the left or the right side of the hand. Violinist and pianist are both aiming at the same ideal of excellence in sound production and musical expression, but the physical contortions leading to it are completely different. In neither case is there a special function for breathing, yet this is a central function for the singer, and the brass and woodwind player, where we find however further sharp distinctions, for instance between the control of vibrating vocal chords, of vibrating lips, and of vibrating reeds, single or double. I posit these kindergarten points of musical science to emphasize the great variety of categories of how sound is made.

If we are contemplating a vast horizon here, this is not to affirm, again, the next 'impossible list'. At least as far as the means of production of musical sound are concerned, a fairly

[3] These comments are gross over-simplifications in order to support a simple point.

small library can embrace however many tens or hundreds of thousands of facts there are about Western classical music, and we sample them as we need: the lay listener may know next to nothing about it without detriment, while the composer will need an exceptional command of these facts. If that were all there is to know, though, there would be little to say about it.

It is clearly not all there is to know, for one articulate musician after another has said, in various ways, that it is not the sound that makes the music. It is something *about* the sound. I am going to attempt to approach that something by illustration and argument, but first I have to admit that in this sphere the Ecstatics have the upper hand, for it will seem impossible to discuss the sound of music without using some sort of metaphor. If as I first stated 'it is impossible to convey in words', then it can only be represented in them. All this is encapsulated by the great conductor (and fine writer) Hermann Scherchen—facts are not enough, there is something else going on, and for this he rekindles the powerful, long-standing metaphor, 'song':

Often we conductors encounter orchestral playing in which all possible virtues—accuracy, elasticity, evenness, power, etc.—are united, but in which we miss one thing: the soul of music, the song that gives inward life to musical sounds.

To sing is the life-function of music. Where there is no singing, the forms of music become distorted and they move in a senseless time-order imposed from without.[4]

Does that help? Do we know what it means to make instrumental music 'sing'? No doubt to some extent it does. Singing is such a natural activity from the nursery to the grave, from joy to lament, and in all its states from humming to ululation, that it does give us an impression, to return to my image from Chapter 1, of how sound is made to 'work' as music. There is nothing wrong with expressing this, in

---

[4] *Handbook of Conducting*, trans. M. D. Calvocoressi (London: Oxford University Press, 1993), 29.

Scherchen's perhaps comforting way, as the giving of 'inward life'.

Nevertheless, there must always be a sense of frustration at trying to capture things in language of that sort. As the authoritative French critic and linguist Roland Barthes asked, 'Are we condemned to the adjective? Are we reduced to the dilemma of either the predictable or the ineffable?' And these were not just rhetorical questions, for Barthes offers a real change of focus. Rather than trying to bend language, to tame it somehow into allowing us to talk about music, let us, he seems to urge, ask questions about music that actually can be answered in words. This, at least, is my paraphrase of what the reader may well find an opaque formulation, which in the interests of accuracy I nevertheless quote here:

> To ascertain whether there are (verbal) means for talking about music without adjectives, it would be necessary to look at more or less the whole of music criticism, something which I believe has never been done. . . . This much, however, can be said: it is not by struggling against the adjective (diverting the adjective you find on the tip of the tongue towards some substantive or verbal periphrasis) that one stands a chance of exorcising musical commentary and liberating it from the fatality of predication; rather than trying to change directly the language on music, it would be better to change the musical object itself, as it presents itself to discourse, better to alter its level of perception or intellection, to displace the fringe of contact between music and language.[5]

I propose to illustrate this in the area of musical balance, the differential quality of musical sound. Balance is worth discussing only at the subtle end of the sonic spectrum. At the gross end lies all the understanding that is obvious—that decent musical sound demands good ensemble (musicians *seeming* to play at the right time and apparently together, as we shall consider further), that at certain dynamic levels one instrument will drown the sound of another, that an off-stage chorus will be faint compared with an on-stage chorus,

[5] *Image-Music-Text*, trans. Stephen Heath (London: Fontana Paperbacks, 1977), 180–1.

that it is when they are in the same register that sounds mask other sounds (thus the piccolo can shriek out from a loud orchestral tutti not by virtue of its volume, but because its notes are above most of the other sound), that the brass player must anticipate the conductor's beat when sitting about twenty metres further from the audience than are the first violins and when the sound travels to the audience at only the same speed (about 760 miles per hour).

At the subtle end, in excellent performance with a well-balanced sound, there is the *illusion* of what musicians call perfect ensemble, but when we ask what that ensemble actually is, it turns out to be its opposite. I would go so far as to say that this is a rule of thumb: perfect ensemble is the impression formed by an essential non-coincidence of sounds measured in microseconds. This rule may be new and surprising to the reader, and to the practising musician it may at first be taken as a heresy, for so much work goes into 'getting music together', timing, rhythmic precision, following the beat, listening to the other players, yet that is to confuse means with ends. If it does seem heretical, I hasten to offer hard evidence. Since the majority of readers will have some awareness of piano music and its performance, and given the happy coincidence that this is where experimental data are available, to that I turn in the next paragraph. To avoid misunderstanding of the above, however, I should say that 'ensemble' embraces not only what I discuss here, but other variables, in particular 'intonation'. Although I shall concentrate on timing, it should be noted that we find a range of 'illusory' phenomena also in the area of what *seems* to be a good distribution of frequencies; in a violin concerto, for instance, the soloist often plays detectably sharp of the orchestra but we *hear* the music as being 'in tune'. Given the wide range of sound production that we throw together in music-making—with fixed-pitch instruments, and the voice and many different 'species' of variable-pitch instruments—it is hardly surprising that throughout modern musical history musicians have studied and written extensively about many different aspects of intonation (and 'tuning').

The illusion of simultaneity while balance is projected by its opposite is quite well known to anyone who has listened to early recordings of pianists who were schooled in the late nineteenth century. It was common, in the 1910s and 1920s when our legacy of recorded sound began, for the bass line in piano music to be made to anticipate the notes above it. Indeed, a short extract from Liszt's étude *Chasse-neige* of 1852 (Ex. 1) shows a case of the precise notation of this effect, where in bar 10 the left hand literally anticipates the right-hand melody—and it's not a matter of the performer choosing (one can find very many examples in the nineteenth-century repertoire of different notations by which, here and there, the composer ties down the pianist in this way).

This was so prevalent, so built into the prevailing style of playing, that by and large treatises of the period don't seem to mention it. Today it is considered old-fashioned and will hardly be tolerated by audiences and recording companies, and pianists are not trained to do it, indeed they are trained *not* to do it except where notated. Yet only a certain amount of listening to recordings where this Romantic technique prevails leads to its assimilation into our sense of musical correctness and—this is the important point—quickly *we cease to be aware of it*. Where has it gone? It is still there physically, but its objective presence has been subsumed into our subjective response. As Scherchen might say, the mere sound has become music, that is, song.

Another Romantic technique, of which I knew but had not really heard in any memorable way until recently, was the spreading of chords (upwards, rapidly, but obviously, when attended to). It is to be heard in performances by Claude Debussy of his own compositions ('The Condon Collection: Claude Achille Debussy', CD 690.07.011, 1992). It is not a feature that I for one have been able to get used to. However, the sense of harmonic richness it seems to generate is remarkable in those of Debussy's recordings like *La Cathédrale engloutie* where one can hear the genius at work, some of them such as 'Dr Gradus' from the 'Children's Corner' Suite being rather obviously not up to scratch.

Ex. 1. Liszt, *Chasse-neige*, bars 8–11

The pianist and Debussy scholar Roy Howat has, I presume deliberately, authentistically, introduced this spread-chord feature into his own performances where, with respect, I am even less able to get used to it!

It is very often by instinct—and I believe will always be much more effectively controlled if it is by intention—that musicians accommodate the need for balance through micro-aural timing. For example, when the piano accompanies a voice or an instrument the conditions of timing can be completely different because of the formant, that is, the beginning of a note. In the voice this is relatively gentle and indistinct and thus the time-lag between it and the relatively crisp, percussive piano note(s) has to be, by how ever many hundredths of a second, longer than in the accompaniment say of an oboe, which has its own crisp formant, and there is a much greater danger of a *perceived* time-lag. Nicholas Cook observes that 'there is a small but general tendency for melodically important instruments to enter slightly before the others',[6] but in my view this is not a tendency so much as an almost omnipresent quality of what is perceived as fine sound in concerted Western music, and certainly in the sound of the piano, where as little as possible is left to the chance of interactions between performers.

Perhaps it is mostly also through instinct that one musician, playing the piano, balances its sound by making fingers and thumbs perform what were until recently mysteries of micro-aural timing. It has been believed but impossible to show that the pianist makes the melody line sing not by making it louder, though this is also a factor, but most pertinently by its micro-aural anticipation of any notes that support it. Thanks to the pioneering work of a psychologist of music, Eric Clarke, we can at last quantify how piano balance works. Ex. 2 is an extract from a Beethoven piano piece designated WoO 60,[7] bars 18–29. Clarke measured in

---

[6] *Music, Imagination, and Culture* (Oxford: Oxford University Press, 1992), 130.

[7] This work without opus number bears no title in Beethoven's manuscript. It is simply designated '*Ziemlich lebhaft*', meaning 'fairly fast'.

Ex. 2. Beethoven, *Klavierstuck* WoO 60, bars 18–29

Note: the numbers (milliseconds) represent the amount by which the
right-hand melody note leads any other note in simultaneity.

+ = lead
− = lag

various performances of these bars on the same piano (a high-quality instrument equipped with photoelectric cells and other measuring devices) the amount of time by which the top note in the right hand preceded any other notes in that simultaneity. Fig. 1 shows the results concerning four performances (numbered 1 to 4) by two players (A and B). Performances 1 and 2 in each case were in response to a request to play 'normally' (and that, of course, means as well as possible). Performances 3 and 4 were in response to a request to play more slowly than normal, though still with the intention of a good interpretation. The pianists were of different nationality, trained in different places. We can see that Player A projects the melody by something like 30 ms (milliseconds) on average. Player B, whose sound will be distinctly different, subjectively, to the listener, projects by less, about 10 ms, one hundredth of a second. But what is so striking is the demonstration here that this is how professionals make the piano sing.[8]

Although we cannot say this was a blind test, I would add that the players knew only that a digital record would be kept and later analysed of various parameters. Thus they were 'under the microscope' and for all we know there may have been a self-conscious attitude in some aspects of the interpretation. What they didn't know, however, is that their means of sound-production could be interpreted from the data. It was only later that some of those concerned realized the significance of the data in this respect. An audio-tape recording of these actual performances sounds, in my opinion, like 'normal' well-balanced piano playing. In *The Musical Mind: The Cognitive Psychology of Music* John Sloboda reports on an experiment written up by R. A. Rasch in 1979 which showed that the violin leading a string trio was doing so literally, with average onset times ahead of the other players of 4–8 ms (p. 100), and Rasch has conducted further experiments on various phenomena of asynchronization. In

---

[8] I am grateful to Professor Eric Clarke of Sheffield University for allowing me to publish this small part of his large programme of experimental research into musical performance.

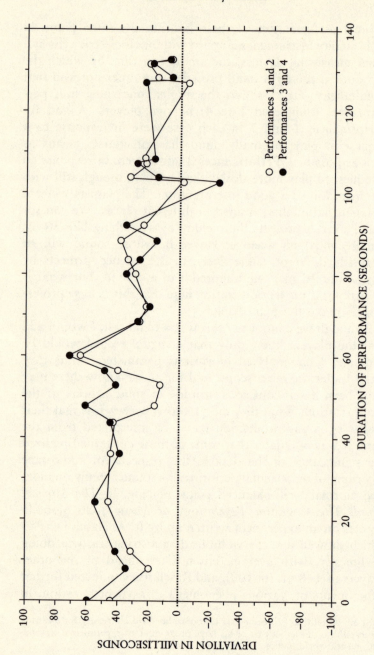

Fig. 1a. Beethoven, WoO 60 extract: Player A

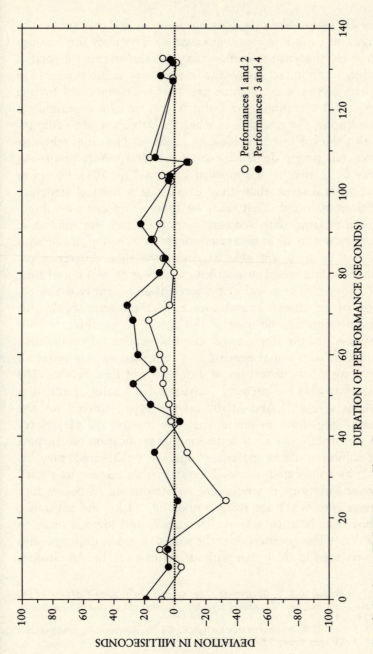

Fig. 1*b*. Beethoven, WoO 60 extract: Player B

his discussion Sloboda does not seem to find this very exciting, and I suppose this is because he is relating the findings to levels of asynchronization that, it is shown experimentally, subjects can in fact judge (the level is tiny—subjects could say which of two sounds came first that were separated by one fiftieth of a second); my point is that, in non-experimental conditions, the question is what the subject is *attending* to. I also think Slobada is looking at the wrong cause when he says that timing deformations of the kind we are discussing may be related 'to the musical structure' (p. 101), except in the general sense that there cannot be a musical structure without a sound. That said, we know from our own directional hearing that auditory response times are miniscule: responding to what is termed 'onset asynchrony' those with normal hearing are able to detect the time difference between sound vibrations striking each ear (a maximum time of about 680 millionths of a second) and identify the direction of an unseen sound source. In the human being this ability begins to be used at the age of about three to four months.[9] In the interests of scientific accuracy I should also add that directional hearing is a function, so it is believed, not only of the detection of differences of time between the ears but also of intensity (obviously, a nearer sound is a louder sound).[10] And finally on this topic, when I say the piano sings I am assuming that this is what the players try to do; strictly, we need some kind of verification on the part of subjects judging 'balanced' against 'unbalanced' playing.

If as I indicated above Roland Barthes advises us to ask better questions in preference to attempting to coerce language into what are really impossible tasks, the substance above has been to act on that advice, and there is more to be done. The question is, is the sound of music illusory—and I have tried to show that without doubt it can be. An illusion,

[9] According to R. S. Illingworth, *The Normal Child: Some Problems of the Early Years and their Treatment* (7th edn., Edinburgh: Churchill Livingstone, 1979), 181.
[10] For an expert account of this see Nils L. Wallin, *Biomusicology* (Stuyvesant, NY: Pendragon Press, 1991), 174 ff.

informally defined, is an effect which induces in us an apperception that we know cannot be the case, not 'really' the case, that is. And I believe that illusion is spread widely in our contact with the sound of music. Consider, for instance, the textural illusion which characterizes that entire repertory of Western tonal music in which the male voice combines with an instrument or instruments. At the beginning of the second song of Schumann's *Dichterliebe*, performed by tenor and piano, what we are 'really' hearing is what is shown in Ex. 3*a*, with the voice forming the bass-line, below the piano. What we perceive, however, is exactly what Schumann wrote in Ex. 3*b*. The convention that a tenor line be printed an octave higher than it physically sounds reflects what does really go on in our minds here and in similar contexts: we hear the left hand of the piano as a bass-line even though it sounds above the voice. Another case of illusion is just as well illustrated from Ex. 3. There are two kinds of sound in this kind of song (and now I mean just song, not song as a metaphor), the sustained and controlled amplitude of the voice and the radical, virtually uncontrolled, thus mechanical melodic decay of the piano notes (once a piano note has been hit, it dies away, for it has no 'breath'). For all that, we take them both to be smooth and in a sense equivalent melodic textures.[11]

The question of what is musical balance is of direct relevance to any discussion of musical performance, but it is not so clear how much importance we must attach to the general idea of illusion in the sound of music. After all, if the performer creates the illusion instinctively as a result of training and of being an insider in this art, and if the listener is there for the subjective ends, not the objective means, that general idea may seem not to have a practical place. Yet I think there is such a place for it. In the illusion of the sound of music, about which its own books could be written, we can find reified, or at least clearly observed, something of the

---

[11] Some of the points in this paragraph are borrowed from my article 'Considerations of Texture', *Music and Letters*, 70/1 (Feb. 1989), 46–57.

Ex. 3. Schumann, *Dichterliebe*, No. 2

mystery of music. The performer conjures: the listener is in
a spell where all is not what it seems.

We should not be in the least surprised to find mystery at
the heart of sound, because sound is a function of time itself,
as I have sought to make explicit from various points of
view. Erwin Stein expresses this interdependency commend-
ably in his discussion of 'The Elements of Musical Sound':

Quite at home as we are in the world of the eye, the realm of the ear
is a fairly strange country. Before the eye things are firm and lasting,

but to the ear everything seems loose and fleeting. Yet it is just these breaks and changes which make aural perception possible. If the sound remained unaltered, it would cease to be felt as a sensation. As light and shade disclose the outlines of a visible object, so the changes of sonority give shape to what we hear. As visible forms are confined in space, so, in the aural sphere, forms exist by their confinement in time, i.e., by the very limitation of their durations. Time is the dimension in which audible objects extend—but time is elusive.[12]

As a result of sound being a *temporal* phenomenon, and of time being so elusive, there is an understandable tendency in performance matters to think of problems of sound statically and thus unhelpfully. Although I can see no way of classifying the aspects of this phenomenon, in practice it is very often by diverting our attention from sound to time that things can be made to work. For example, one frequently encounters among string players who use vibrato in the modern manner an awareness that the sound is improvable, because there is some lack of (an ideal) smoothness, something a touch rough about it. Nearly always this can be corrected when the player is encouraged to regard this as a temporal problem rather than concentrating on the purely sonic result. The problem is that the vibrato is not starting from the very beginning of each note. The player *feels* that it is, and because the player is actively making the sound by the placing of a finger on the fingerboard and then its subtle movement to vary the pitch, all sense of micro-time is lost. But to the listener, that microsecond which makes the onset of the vibrato late may as well be a whole second, for we perceive these things (without necessarily knowing it) categorically as part of the sound: half a second? a tenth of a second?—this matters not. 'Late' is what matters, and it can unlock a solution that will never emerge from thinking only about sonic 'roughness'.[13]

[12] *Form and Performance* (London: Faber and Faber, 1962), 23.
[13] There are many competing theories of playing the violin family which lie behind the different teaching methods, and some experts may reject this particular point; all I can say is that it is based on years of close observation of talented student players alongside the brilliant professionals it has been my privilege to know.

Another and quite incontrovertible general case is when certain parts of a performance seem, subjectively, too loud. It may well be that there has been a sonic misjudgement by the player. Nine out of ten times when this happens, however, it will be found that a crescendo has been made, as required by the composer's notation, but made too soon. In singing and with most acoustic (non-electronic) instruments a crescendo results from an increasing physical effort. This motor acceleration is in conflict with the metrical regularity that (in a lot of music) enables us to keep track of the musical motion in time. So we cease attending to the metrical grid in order to effect something that must go increasingly quicker than that grid—the increasing physical effort that will yield the crescendo—and thus a temporal problem turns into a sonic, dynamic result ('dynamic' in its musical sense of relative loud and soft, but in origin dynamic too in its dictionary sense of 'force producing motion'). It's not our hearing that is a problem, but the difficulty of running two internal clocks, one ticking regularly to the time of the music, the other, serving our autonomic nervous system, having to accelerate; no doubt the anxiety I discussed in Chapter 3 cannot but exacerbate the difficulty of getting the balance right. What seems to me to make it incontrovertible that we are dealing with a dislocation of temporal, not sonic perception is the following remarkable fact. It is obvious that for strictly physical, motor reasons people will tend to speed up in crescendos and slow down in diminuendos unless they make the necessary (whether instinctive or trained doesn't matter here) correction for this: you can hear this correction missing in less than highly skilled performance. But in my experience, when diminuendos are misplaced, like crescendos they also tend to be, not too late as 'motor' logic would suggest (except, for instance, in the case of wind and brass players who may speed up as well as running out of volume when running out of breath), but too soon. Assuming the empirical evidence is what I believe it to be, I don't think any further proof is needed: we are talking about 'too-soon-ness', not 'poor-sound-ness'—about timing.

Would Roland Barthes frown at the thought that sound 'is' in some sense time? It may be he would, for 'time' is just another noun (he speaks of the 'adjective', but 'noun' does just as well here, I feel). It is a noun however, that we are *used* to, that we cannot do without in everyday life as in art. 'Time is only an abstraction from happening; time makes sense only when there is something going on by which to tick it off'[14] and the sound of music is some such thing.

[14] W. V. Quine, *Quiddities: An Intermittently Philosophical Dictionary* (Harmondsworth: Penguin Books, 1990), 38.

7

Design in Music

> We have witnessed an abundant crop of more or less absurd
> analyses which, under various pretexts—phenomenological,
> statistical, etc.—have ended in debasement and lamentable
> caricature.
>
> (Pierre Boulez, *Boulez on Music Today*)

Near the beginning of the first chapter I indicated that there
are cases where an improved theoretical understanding of
music is bound to be useful in such circumstances as complex harmony, refractory text, or weak composition. I want
now to ask what are the general features of music that are
amenable to conceptual and when possible theoretical understanding, that is, to some further purpose.

A word of explanation is needed about why one has to be
so emphatic about this. As the study of music using what
have come to be called analytical techniques has flowered in
recent decades (or, some would say, has spread like a dis-
ease), so the debate has burgeoned about what these techniques are *for*. I mean 'for' in both senses: not only as to
purpose; but what do these techniques seek to represent?
With what do they side? Boulez complains that 'we are
swamped with vast tables of ridiculous symbols, reflections
of a void, timetables of trains which will never leave!'[1] So,
he is saying, all this represents *nothing at all*. It is not even
of interest to ask why, then, people indulge in it. People
watch television too. So what?[2] I am presenting this matter

[1] *Boulez on Music Today*, trans. S. Bradshaw and R. Rodney Bennett (London: Faber and Faber, 1975), 17.
[2] I do not propose to comment here on the vast tracts of print that have
formed a sort of 'meta-analytical' debate in modern musicology. But, not to
over-simplify, I do believe that there is a strong 'activity that is its own reward'

briefly in the dismissive spirit in which Boulez expounds at greater length in order to induce a sense of relief, for there is an alternative, Boulez goes on to insist. He called it an ' "active" analytical method' and described, in moving words that remind me of Hoffmann on Beethoven (see above), what such method is for:

Is the composer then only a pretext? Michel Butor, at the end of his essay on Baudelaire, gives a definitive answer to this objection. 'Some people', he writes, 'may think that, while intending to write about Baudelaire, I have only succeeded in speaking of myself. It would certainly be better to say that it was Baudelaire who spoke of me. *He speaks of you*'. If you question the masters of an earlier period with perseverance and conviction you become the medium of their replies: they speak of you through you.[3]

Perhaps there is irony in the fact that whereas the intellectual with a carefully nurtured philosophical disposition may well find Boulez's notion of past masters 'speaking of us through us' altogether too gooey for our own good, this is just what the performer does experience when things are going well; and this is something of what passes to the audience—'it's just as if Mozart himself had been playing tonight', we sometimes say.

This kind of handing-on—a kind of immortality for the composers of course, though not one in which we are aware they can take any eventual satisfaction—is a handing-on not just of experience, but also of knowledge: not just of magic (which is what we're really after), but of how the tricks are done. I argued above (see pp. 34–5) that one of the problems in music is our tendency to prefer not to know how the tricks are done because then we'll lose the sense of magic. It wasn't suited to my narrative to take the argument further at that stage, but now it is time to explain that we will never lose the magic by knowing how the tricks are done. It's an

argument, which was considered in my article 'Music Analysis: Commentaries', in J. Paynter *et al.* (eds.), *Compendium of Contemporary Musical Thought* (London: Routledge, 1992), 634–49.

[3] *Boulez on Music Today*, 18–19.

unending chain. You see the trick; but where did the idea of doing it come from in the first place? And so on. I do not believe art can ever lose its mystery when there is quality and when there is what I can only call sanity. We have a sense of *change* as the tricks reveal themselves, but with each step towards further understanding we see that there are further mysteries beyond our new, more distant horizon.

I hope this will have provided credibility for the assertion that music is in part a transmission of what I am calling design. It is no threat; on the contrary, it sustains us in the journey to discover more about art. Design approximates to what is usually understood as form in music, but I think the work 'design' keeps the composer in our minds in a constructive way. I know that in talking about design I shall not avoid being dubbed a formalist by those who have turned their face against notions of structure, but I can live with that. I even dare to say, in one further moment of futurism, that the postmodern antagonism towards notions of autonomous structure will perish in its own neurosis.

'Structure' is always depicted as the most difficult aspect of musical design to discuss in a simple way. I do not see why this is necessarily the case and feel it comes down to finding the right analogies within people's other experience. This becomes more difficult, of course, at extremes of technicality, so it will always require monographs (even those free of Boulez's 'ridiculous symbols') to respond to the performing musician who says 'I just don't know what you mean when you say that in this movement there is a middleground bass arpeggiation using mixture and reduplicating the scale-steps of the background' . . . 'and I don't know what you mean when you tell me that this other piece is controlled by a connected set complex bound by a hexachord and a secondary nexus pentachord' . . . 'and I'm stumped when you complain that it's obvious from my performance of this character in Wagner that I've failed to hear the unsung voice of the narrative *and* didn't realize that I'm supposed to be androgynous all the way through' . . . and so on.

I am not going to shirk exposing some more difficult ideas, but first let us ask what is musical structure, which I can only answer by saying what it is like—narrative. Anyone who wants to know what a 'tonic' is in major-minor 'tonal' music has only to think of the theatre. When Desdemona is alone on stage, or with Iago, or Iago and Cassio are on stage, and when all the other like monologues, dialogues, overhearings, and ensembles are conducted, *where is Othello*? He is the 'tonic': he will return and we know this though we won't wish to think about it consciously or we'll miss the other things that are going on *now*; these ongoing things are going on *because* of the existence, nature, and history of Othello himself.[4]

'Tonics' aside, structure is surely easy to conceptualize when it comes down to musical themes. When in the course of Tchaikovsky's Fifth Symphony we hear its second theme (Ex. 4*a*) we are not thinking, 'Wonder where *this* has gone and what it's up to at the moment?' (Ex. 4*b*). We *know* that Ex. 4*b* will come back in some form, if not how, if not when. Consider an example that appropriates our sense of structure by working against it. Over the years critics have enjoyed discussing Tchaikovsky's First Piano Concerto, which opens with the majestic theme everyone can recognize or hum: startlingly, the theme is never heard again. It is an outstanding example of a composer's design against what we expect. '*That*'ll make you think,' I suppose Tchaikovsky may have said contemplating his design and its future that he could not live directly to experience. Recall Boulez's words: 'I speak of you through you'. (I don't need to append references to the literature to assert, as is easily exemplified, that all the later themes of this concerto transform or can in some other way he analytically related to Tchaikovsky's

---

[4] This is not supposed to be a contribution to Shakespeare criticism. Obviously the dramatic voices are much more complex because there is *hierarchy* (not so low down in this hierarchy, for instance, is that stark 'character' which has such a presence in the play, the handkerchief!) and there is *ambiguity*, here in particular, as Verdi and Boito had to puzzle out, whether the play is not really 'about' Iago.

Ex. 4*a*. Tchaikovsky, Fifth Symphony, 1st mvt., 2nd subject

Ex. 4*b*. Tchaikovsky, Fifth Symphony, 1st mvt., 1st subject

opening salvo. This would amount to proving that this piece of music as a whole makes sense thematically, and it would be odd to think that a work that makes no sense had endured in our culture for well over a century. 'What people think' is that the opening theme stands *alone*. Tchaikovsky came up with the exception that proves the rule.)

Design is so important that the musician really cannot afford to be unaware of it. Formal 'repeat marks' offer many cases where performers think they have an option to ignore the composer's instructions and in doing so damage the composer's design and thus the listener's enjoyment.[5] Similarly, performances are often spoiled at the end because whoever is performing or directing a performance doesn't grasp the music's own self-closure. Stein puts this very well, although we must be wary of his implication that everything the performer needs to know is there in the notes on the page:

Our sense of form demands a reason why music, the phenomenon of sound which has been projected into time—whether for five minutes

---

[5] I considered this problem in detail in 'The Formal Repeat', *Journal of the Royal Musical Association*, 112/2 (1987), 198–207.

or an hour makes no basic difference—suddenly ceases. The feeling that the form has been completed is created by such means as the loosening and, finally, the disintegration of the structure; a definite final statement, or the dying away of the sound. The performer has to shape the music accordingly, and the slowing down of the tempo is only one of the means, and the most obvious, of bringing a piece to a halt. It cannot be often enough emphasized that the stereotyped exaggeration of *ritardandos* at the end is a bad mannerism. The fact that the music closes down should not be emphasized to a degree which distorts the features of the structure. Often a *ritardando* is composed and written out in broadening note-values, and often there are other features, such as a series of strong cadences, which make any additional *ritardando* superfluous, and therefore inadmissible. It is bad musical manners to stress what is made sufficiently plain by the notes.[6]

I am equally struck by what Christopher Wintle wrote in 1982, about new music (that is, newish), when he seems to complain that design has not been assimilated. Writing about Webern's Concerto, Op. 24, of which he has presented some detailed analysis, he concludes in part:

It may still be the case that a conductor need not acquire all the information assembled in this paper before lifting his baton. Nevertheless, it is striking that in the available commercial recordings of the Concerto, so little comprehension of structure is evinced. Dynamics are ignored, phrasing is under-articulated, tempo gradations are over-ridden, and the whole deprived of the sense of directed motion that alone can bring this music to life. Instead, we are offered too often that which is chic, clean, inorganic and dead.[7]

Wintle's words 'inorganic and dead' are telling indeed and lead us on to the second general point in this chapter, that musical design has to be *animated* in performance, it has to be brought to life, *re*-created. Summoning music into presence is a difficult notion to encapsulate: even philosopher Mary Warnock has to resort to indication rather than formulation—'It is at any rate certain that we will *not* be satisfied

[6] *Form and Performance* (London: Faber and Faber, 1962), 71–2.
[7] 'Analysis and Performance: Webern's Concerto Op. 24/ii', *Music Analysis*, 1/1 (Mar. 1982), 73–99; p. 98.

unless we have also succeeded in producing in ourselves the particular, though probably inexpressible, "feel" that the absent thing would have if we were actually in its presence'.[8] We can gain a strong sense of this summoning up, however, by again resorting to the analogy of drama; we can understand this in the sense of Mr Actor who animates *Othello*; and in fact in bringing Othello to life to play his part in the design fixed by Shakespeare an intriguing displacement takes place, for Mr Actor disappears. Where is he when Othello confronts us with his pomp and murderous jealousy? Nowhere at all. We see the same as we are drawn in to the fantastic world of the marionette. Once we believe it lives, where is the puppeteer? 'What strings?' we would ask before the spell is broken. Speaking in musicianly terms, Wintle bemoans a lack of 'directed motion', and these are interesting words. I have already tried to establish that time is of the essence in music, it is what yields sound, or we can say that sound can't exist outside it, and this seems to equate with the idea of 'motion'. Music seems to take on a motion of its own.

I am going to try to expose some of this kind of 'work' in respect of Ex. 5, 'Lento' by Stravinsky. I have chosen this (haunting) example on the grounds that it is simple, performable by anyone with a rudimentary ability to read music at the piano; but it is not a 'slight' work, as anyone may be forgiven for thinking at first sight, even first hearing, and I need to first establish its status as a work of art. It is the sixth of eight short piano pieces by Stravinsky entitled *Les Cinq Doigts*. He composed and in 1922 published this music, and these facts should endow cultural authority to a score that might otherwise be thought trite, or at least inconsequential. Further suspicion is raised by the title, and by the indications of hand position placed over the first and the two last systems. Immediately we will ask ourselves whether this is not 'merely' music for children, in a pedagogical tradition of easy, single-hand-position pieces that embraces

---

[8] *Imagination* (London: Faber and Faber, 1980), 173.

Diabelli in the early days of pianism two hundred years ago, or Bartók, say, in the first *Mikrokosmos* volume of 1940, and any number of piano tutor volumes nowadays. But then, Stravinsky did have a permutational turn of mind. Eric Walter White notes in his classic book *Stravinsky: The Composer and his Works* that we are looking at 'a foretaste of other more complicated series to be used [by Stravinsky] a third of a century later!'[9] And if we are looking for further credibility, bear in mind that, just as at around this time Stravinsky was orchestrating the 'Five Easy Pieces' for piano duet of 1916–17, so too in the early 1960s he was to return to *Les Cinq Doigts*, reworking them a little, reordering, transposing, adding here and there, to produce the 'Eight Instrumental Miniatures' premièred in Toronto in 1962, Stravinsky conducting the CBC Symphony Orchestra. If I haven't yet put this piece into a sufficient frame of reference, I appeal to a compelling essay by Jacques Derrida in his book *Spurs*, where the author asks why on earth the fragment 'I have forgotten my umbrella', written by Friedrich Nietzsche, placed in quotation marks and signed, was not included in the *Complete Works*.[10] How can this not be a work?, asks Derrida. It is signed and in quotation marks, and anyway, as Derrida notes as the point of embarkation for this rich literary-critical essay, of course something must have *reminded* Nietzsche that he had forgotten his umbrella. What might that have been? Thus begins the kind of train of interpretative thought that we customarily apply to *Macbeth*, or to *Tristram Shandy*, enshrining the work in a cultural canon, not anxiously, but lending it some influence. In fact, unlike Nietzsche's line, Ex. 5 is not even a 'fragment' in the traditional sense of the word, but a complete, rounded 'work' of musical narrative.

Because even with a short piece of music like this the opportunities for contemplation are limitless, I shall restrict what follows to the examination of Stravinsky's performance indications—obviously, playing the notated pitches

---

[9] (London: Faber and Faber 1979), 298.
[10] *Spurs: Nietzsche's Styles*, trans. Barbara Harlow (Chicago: University of Chicago Press, 1979), 122–43.

Ex. 5. Stravinsky, 'Lento', from *Les Cinq Doigts*

Lento

Ex. 6. Simple analysis of melody of Ex. 5, bars 1–4

metronomically in correct order is not going to animate this music. Stravinsky himself spoke of 'hidden elements', and 'the realization of these elements is . . . a matter of experience and intuition, in a word, of the talent of the person who is called upon to present the music'.[11]

Clearly there is a degree of accentual complexity within the 3/4 metre. If it can be agreed that the first phrase of the melody ends with the completion of a stepwise descent from dominant to tonic, the first melodic unit of the piece can be picked out as in Ex. 6. Note that this covers essentially *three* bars (admittedly, held over into the next bar), an 'irregular' number against the backdrop of Classical and Romantic phrasing which tends to be in two-, four-, and eight-bar groupings (Schoenberg called this the 'aesthetic' of the eight-bar phrase). Irregularity is heightened in what follows, with three *five*-beat melodic units (bars 4^2–5^3, 6–7^2 and 7^3–9^1—as we shall see, however, something else intervenes at the end of bar 8). Against this the left hand counterpoints groups of crotchets that also cut across the barlines—3, 4, 3, 4, 4, 4— the first two pairs perhaps setting up a larger sense of grouping in *seven*. These innocent-looking lines offer a kaleidoscope of prime numbers, a lack of coincidence between different strands of musical organization. Stravinsky's phrase marks will be of exceptional importance in making sense of this design, and I think he uses them initially to animate the 3/4 metre which must be present for the other numbers to work

[11] *Poetics of Music* (Cambridge, Mass.: Harvard University Press, 1942), 123.

Ex. 7. Harmonic background to Ex. 5

against; thus in the first six bars each down-beat attack is stressed, in particular those at bars 5 and 6 when the cumulative metrical disruption most needs its expressive counterbalance. If we look at the counterpoint of right- and left hand phrase-initiation and accentuation up to bar 8^2, it requires quite some attention, and subtlety, in performance— if the puppet is to move fluently rather than in a series of jerks:

```
beat 1 X X | 4 X X | 7 X X | 10 X X | 13 X X | 16 X X | 19 X X | 22 X X
RH  >       >       >              >       >              >
LH  >       >       >       >              >       >       >       >
```

One of the narcotic pleasures of this music is the shift of scale in the middle section (bars 9–13), where the harmony changes from the prolongation of a D-based sonority to what I take to be a sustained supertonic sonority, so that the harmonic background of the piece is something like Ex. 7 (just as we may summarize the plot of a play). If Ex. 7 is approximately what the listener senses of the harmonic design overall, the mobile (yearning?) quality of the fifth-finger Cs in bars 9 and 11 finds some technical explanation, for C is an appoggiatura, what is sometimes called in British terminology a 'leaning note', which *must* resolve downwards in common practice musical convention. We see again here how Stravinsky asks the performer to tip the metrical balance into 3/4 with phrase marks on the downbeats of bars 10 and 12.

There are two particularly interesting features here. The first is the accent notated in the right hand of bar 8, a sign of intrusion and initiation. It is intrusive because the basic metrical unit of the music has been the crotchet, subdivided though it may be by quavers, semiquavers, and, in the left hand of bars 6–8^1, rests of indeterminate length (they depend on what duration the performer gives to the staccato Gs in the bass). This accent on the final quaver of bar 8 catches our attention, like, say, a bird that darts into our peripheral vision. And like the knock of the stick at the beginning of a Japanese play (a device that has in fact been adopted by various contemporary Western composers—beginning or ending a piece of music with a loud percussion has become a cliché, though one that composers can still use effectively), the accent launches us into a new part of the drama. Every other D that marks a phrase ending is, literally, phrased off by Stravinsky's instructions (bars 3^3, 5^3, 7^1, 16^3 and, finally, 18^3): but this D is picked out for a structural role that the performer must somehow acknowledge (not that it's difficult) in order to present the composer's design.

Secondly, note the exceptionally long phrase mark over the left hand in bars 9–13^2. I doubt that this represents phrasing in the sense that all the other slurs in the piece do, a melodic 'shaping' (each phrase having a dynamic focus and dying away, however slightly, as it closes). This particular mark is surely cautionary rather than active. Through it Stravinsky says, 'play this smoothly: do not *articulate* the left hand in any way; this middle section has to be animated in a way that is distinct from what precedes and follows'. There is every reason to think of it as an analytical marking: 'this is one single unit of the design and must not be subdivided by the performer'. I am not saying that Stravinsky is doing anything particularly novel with this kind of instruction—Chopin, for instance, often wrote phrase marks covering dozens of bars that are clearly nothing other than conceptual guides to the performer about the articulation of the musical form.[12] But it is revealing to see the care with which the composer's guidance is passed on and must be interpreted.

---

[12] See e.g. the facsimile edition of Chopin's holograph of the Second Ballade, published by the Fryderyk Chopin Institute, Warsaw.

Having enthused about the accent in bar 8, I shall have to try to address the tenuto or stress mark over the left-hand A at bar 5^3. We might think that it is the kind of stress which the 'couplet' phrase mark over the bar to a staccato note already conveys. Again, then, perhaps it is cautionary, and to some extent analytical ('new development in the left hand: lean on it with the left-hand thumb, because you might not be prepared to do this off your own bat on a third, weak beat of the bar'). I think, however, that there is a deeper aspect to this which threatens to open up a different area of discussion. Briefly, this note A is going to play a dramatic role at the end of the piece. It *is* the end (bars 18^3–19), and defiant because it unites closure with expectancy (it is the dominant of the scale, a pitch that is normally unsuitable for supporting a closing harmony, and in forcing it to function thus Stravinsky asks—rather as I described my imagined Tchaikovsky above—'Well, what do you think of that?!'). I believe that Stravinsky prefigures this towards the end of the first part of the piece and *this* is the real function of the stress on A in bar 5^3. The different area of discussion, then, is how composers build design into music that, in a sense, there is nothing the performer can do anything about, other than knowing it is there. In recapitulatory forms, for example (often in Schubert, also, say, the Brahms Rhapsody in B minor, Op. 79 No. 1), composers will sometimes make a tiny change to material that is being repeated from the exposition but will lead into new or transposed material in the recapitulation. I think these are cases of deliberate inconsistency, a way for the composer and performers to keep track of the musical structure, imperceptibly to the listener except that the general shape of the movement will be enhanced.[13]

I trust it will be clear that this excursus into the detail of

[13] I say 'I think' for two reasons: first, I am not aware that this subject has been fully discussed in the literature; secondly, it is not something of which I have made a systematic investigation—but it is certainly to be found, and perhaps originates in Haydn and Mozart, although it is not clear who learned it from whom. The extensive recent literature on discrepancies in the manuscripts and publications of 18th-c. composers has not, in my view, led to any general understanding of this particular feature.

how a musical design has to be animated through the composer's instructions (where there are instructions) represents
a general feature, according to my intention announced on
p. 79. There can surely be no doubt that this sort of examination is not self-gratifying, or not only self-gratifying, and
not only does it have the obvious purpose of bringing the
music to life, but it is *necessary* for that animation. The skilled
performer sight-reading Stravinsky's score may pick this all
up instinctively, being as it were 'played' by all of the composer's visual cues without giving them any thought, any
existence other than their reification in the relationship between musical sounds. This can happen, however, only in
relatively simple cases. The skilled musician will know that
most musical scores contain an immense amount of information that it takes time and introspection to master, and this
is partly what practice and rehearsal are about—what does
it mean? and how do I do it? I hope that the lay reader, however, will have gained a little insight into, as I have said before,
what performers have to think about.

When looking through the microscope in this way, it is
easy to lose sight of the enormous difference in musical scope,
between the factors in play with a little piece by Stravinsky,
and those that arise in the extensive designs of very large-
scale works. It is barely possible to generalize about interpretative factors in large-scale works, other than to make the
various rather obvious points: for instance, that the 'organic'
shapes of Romantic music (with their familiar characteristics
to which the listener responds with the comfort of *recognition*—in the finales of most concertos, for example, there is
usually an increase in tempo which acts as a signpost to the
end) have given way in the twentieth century to a great
diversity of large-scale patterns—be they the kind of huge,
repetitive 'frescos' familiar from Boulez including his current large and evolving work *Répons* for instrumental ensemble, soloists, and electro-acoustic equipment (first heard
in 1981), Stockhausen's 'moment' forms, or, say, the large
minimalist 'collage' forms such as Steve Reich's *Different
Trains* (1988).

Given the diversity of large-scale patterns, the unpredictability of overall designs, I suppose that what the musicologist Hermann Kretzschmar wrote in 1903 has become *more* rather than less true of new music:

a large composition will never become a work of art unless the composer goes beyond his first ideas and penetrates from the sphere of the unconscious to a clear understanding of the nature and true end of those first ideas. Philosophers repeatedly overlook this cardinal point in the composer's activity, and in so doing they reveal their ignorance of the very essence of creativity . . . Exceptional [compositional] results are the outcome of calculation and conscious invention rather than mere inspiration . . . And the same is true of the listener too. It is only enthusiastic amateurs who are content to make their enigmatic character the distinguishing feature of musical impressions . . . Any serious and gifted music-lover must progress beyond that first stage, both in his listening and in his attempts to understand what he hears. Even a knowledge and understanding of musical forms of all kinds is no more than a step on the road.[14]

'A large composition will never become a work of art' unless the *performance* too shows a penetration to the 'true end' of the musical design, and I cannot but agree that we have to understand 'musical forms of all kinds'; but as I said, it is hard to generalize about how this understanding is translated into musical action. What we know is that without it, design is lost. Witness Sergey Rakhmaninov, who believed that the performance of any piece of music requires one to know where is its 'culminating point':

This culmination, depending on the actual piece, may be at the end or in the middle, it may be loud or soft; but the performer must know how to approach it with absolute calculation, absolute precision, because if it slips by, then the whole construction crumbles, the piece becomes disjointed and scrappy and does not convey to the listener what must be conveyed.[15]

---

[14] 'A Stimulus to Promote a Hermeneutics of Music' quoted from Bojan Bujić (ed.), *Music in European Thought 1851–1912* (Cambridge: Cambridge University Press, 1988), 120.
[15] G. Norris, *Rachmaninoff* (London: J. M. Dent, 1993), 78.

I do like those words 'the whole construction crumbles': there is something deeply reassuring in reading in Rakhmaninov words that would have done any 1960s Parisian structuralist proud.

To the extent that I have implied here that it is easier to study details of design than design overall I may seem to be stating the obvious, but in fact I have tried to avoid that implication for two reasons. First, I don't see how you really can understand a detail of design unless it conforms to a conception of the musical work as a whole. One might 'deconstruct' all my seemingly almost factual observations above about Stravinsky's 'Lento' to expose layer upon layer of music-ideological tissue—that music is all of a piece, that the whole is greater than the sum of its parts but *depends* on them for its very existence, that the text has to be regarded as 'perfect' (for all that I wanted to ban this word in Chapter 1) at least in the sense that Stravinsky has written nothing here however tiny that is intended to *mislead* any of us in any way, and so on to the end of my last endless list. When now and again I hear people say silly things—well, things I can't agree with—about musical detail there is never any difficulty in finding the *wider* 'structural' reason for the disagreement when it concerns music that is integrated, music that is not itself designed to be subversive (as it must be recognized some music is). Secondly, I would be the last to downgrade music analysis as a key to 'structure' which has, as Nicholas Cook reminds us in *A Guide to Musical Analysis*, an important role to play in today's musical culture:

It has this role because the ability to set aside details and 'see' large-scale connections appropriate to the particular musical context, which is what analysis encourages, is an essential part of the musician's way of perceiving musical sound. For the performer, it is obvious that analysis has a role to play in the memorization of extended scores, and to some extent in the judgment of large-scale dynamic and rhythmic relationships (although some of the claims that Schenkerian analysis, in particular, is indispensable for performers and conductors have surely been overstated).[16]

[16] London: J. M. Dent and Sons, 1989), 232.

It is possible to ideate, to conceive, 'the piece of music as a whole'. Just as the composer draws the line and decides that 'I have finished this piece and will send it to the publisher',[17] so the music analyst has to come to a view for a particular purpose, and so the performer is always bound to the thought, 'here we go, *this is it*', and so the listener knows 'well, *that was that*'.

'Magic', 'mystery', and suchlike have been mentioned before, but I would say finally here that what it all comes down to, what the performer and the audience are both hoping to find through the design of music, and often they do, is plenitude—the condition of being absolutely full or complete, as the dictionary says. Where we can find plenitude, which is what music offers to those who play and to those who listen, and bearing in mind how significant music is in so many ways in so many lives, all shall be well.

[17] Many composers, as is well known, go on tinkering, never quite willing to let the work go, such as Mendelssohn and Brahms. It is probably typical of Western composers since the Baroque period to cling on to rethinking—even Mozart, so apparently Bach-like in his relentless moving on from one idea to the next, also took time to rework original material. Twentieth-century composers have been no different. A world in which Stravinsky revised *The Rite of Spring* is a world of continuity, just as Joyce redrafted *Portrait of the Artist as a Young Man* at least four times.

Postscript

I have referred several times, at what I regard as key points, to the fact that art offers us different kinds of experience. For all that I stick to my stab at Larkin at the beginning of the Introduction, I did not question the fact that an image and its working-out are not the same. For all that I have tried to encourage people to think about the connections between performance and all the things we do when we are not performing or experiencing the result, again the distinction is recognized. Arnold Whittall asked me whether I had 'done full justice to what "real" performance is, or can be', and in closing, first I seek to answer that question briefly.

There are two answers, on different levels. It almost goes without saying that the 'reality' of performance can be documented at great length, be it about how to cope with arc-lights (wear light clothes!) and what people make of beta-blockers, or, say, about whether as a performer one can and should invest the time in learning contemporary techniques that may not endure, and in how to play 'period' instruments of which audiences are likely to tire (if those geniuses of the workshop who came up with 'modern' instruments—Boehm, Sax, Steinway, and the rest—knew what they were doing). The whole question of attitude comes into this too: *Must* we read the memoirs of performers—Artur Rubinstein's, for instance—in order to get to the reality of musical performance? Reality in this sense, it seems to me, is a kind of fiction or temporary know-how. I do not denigrate it, but not many know how to deal with it; anyhow, their reality is as real as anyone else's. Like performers, listeners want an experience, not anything provisional. I hope to have covered all of this in principle.

At another level, however, and this is my second answer, the event and its documentation are not the same and never can be. 'Real' musical performance in this sense is just what it says it is, and obviously it does not take place in books like this one, or anywhere else outside its own domain. We shouldn't be alarmed about this, which is a fact of life. By and large, poetry is read and thought about, though there is an obvious push uniting Homer with 'Rap' to make it a present, performed experience. By and large, music is a present, performed experience, the living art that mid-twentieth-century linguists identified as being uniquely like language because it cannot exist but in time, though it has been 'read' and thought about since time immemorial. To denigrate the inner ear is ridiculous. It is all Beethoven had.

Secondly, finally, I have rather glossed over the difficulties people continue to encounter in deciding what is and what is not music in present-day Western culture. I have the feeling nowadays that the musical 'modernism' rife and so fascinating in my own formative years was a pre-technological phenomenon. The whole distinction between 'high-art' and 'popular' music is of course breaking down; as the social historians describe, you can see this in everyday life, where technology replaces humanity.

Yet in the end it doesn't. I don't think the public is ready to give up classical music for uni-beat LPO sound bites, or for bits from the operas sung by as many as three decent(ish) tenors. We are certainly not ready to give up Beethoven, and thus one has to practise at an acoustic instrument, and listen to and read scores carefully, concentrating. Giving up Schoenberg and Stravinsky, Messiaen and Bartók, would also be fruitless self-denial, but it takes a lot of work and thought among practitioners to bring about continuity and expertise, which is what this book is about.

Bibliography

ARISTOTLE, *The Ethics*, trans. J. A. K. Thomson (Harmondsworth: Penguin, 1983).

BACH, C. P. E., *Essay on the True Art of Playing Keyboard Instruments*, trans. W. J. Mitchell (London: Eulenberg, 1974).

BARTHES, R., *Image-Music-Text*, trans. S. Heath (London: Fontana Paperbacks, 1977).

BERRY, W., *Musical Structure and Performance* (New Haven, Conn.: Yale University Press, 1989).

BLOOM, H., *The Anxiety of Influence* (Oxford: Oxford University Press, 1973).

BOULEZ, P., *Boulez on Music Today*, trans. S. Bradshaw and R. Rodney Bennett (London: Faber and Faber, 1975; first published 1971).

BUJIĆ, B. (ed.), *Music in European Thought 1851–1912* (Cambridge: Cambridge University Press, 1988).

CONE, E. T., *Musical Form and Musical Performance* (New York: Norton, 1968).

—— 'Musical Form and Musical Performance Reconsidered', *Music Theory Spectrum*, 7 (1985), 149–58.

COOK, N., *A Guide to Musical Analysis* (London: J. M. Dent and Sons, 1989; first published 1987).

—— *Music, Imagination, and Culture* (Oxford: Oxford University Press, 1992).

DART, T., *The Interpretation of Music* (4th edn., London: Hutchinson, 1967; first published 1954).

DERRIDA, J., *Spurs: Nietzsche's Styles*, trans. B. Harlow (Chicago: University of Chicago Press, 1979).

DUNSBY, J. M., 'The Formal Repeat', *Journal of the Royal Musical Association*, 112/2 (1987), 198–207.

—— 'Analysis and Performance', *Music Analysis*, 8/1–2 (1989), 5–20.

—— 'Considerations of Texture', *Music and Letters*, 70/1 (1989), 46–57.

—— 'Music Analysis: Commentaries', in J. Paynter *et al.* (eds.), *Compendium of Contemporary Musical Thought* (London: Routledge, 1992), 634–49.

FREUD, S., *Introductory Lectures on Psychoanalysis*, trans. J. Strachey (Harmondsworth: Penguin, 1973).

GOULD, G., *The Glenn Gould Reader*, ed. T. Page (London: Faber and Faber, 1987).

GREEN, B., with GALLWEY, W. T. *The Inner Game of Music* (London: Pan, 1987).

GRIFFITHS, P., *A Concise History of Modern Music* (London: Thames and Hudson, 1978).

ILLINGWORTH, R. S., *The Normal Child: Some Problems of the Early Years and their Treatment* (7th. edn., Edinburgh: Churchill Livingstone, 1979).

KELLER, HANS, *Criticism*, trans. L. Gerdine (London: Faber and Faber, 1987).

KELLER, HERMANN, *Phrasing and Articulation* (London: Barrie and Rockliff, 1966).

KERMAN, J., *Musicology* (London: Fontana Paperbacks, 1985).

KRAUS, K., *Half-Truths and One-and-a-Half Truths* (New York: Carcanet Press, 1986).

LE HURAY, P., *Authenticity in Performance: Eighteenth-Century Case Studies* (Cambridge: Cambridge University Press, 1990).

LEPPERT, R., and MCCLARY, S. (eds.), *Music and Society: The Politics of Composition, Performance and Reception* (Cambridge: Cambridge University Press, 1987).

LEVINSON, J., *Music, Art, and Metaphysics* (Ithaca, NY: Cornell University Press, 1990).

MCCLARY, S., *Feminine Endings: Music, Gender, and Sexuality* (Minneapolis: University of Minnesota Press, 1991).

MEYER, L., *Music, the Arts, and Ideas: Patterns and Predictions in Twentieth-Century Culture* (Chicago: University of Chicago Press, 1967).

NARMOUR, E., 'On the Relationship of Analytical Theory to Performance and Interpretation', in E. Narmour and R. Solie (eds.), *Explorations in Music, the Arts, and Ideas* (Stuyvesant, NY: Pendragon Press, 1988).

NORRIS, G., *Rachmaninoff* (2nd edn., London: J. M. Dent, 1993).

QUINE, W. V., *Quiddities: An Intermittently Philosophical Dictionary* (Harmondsworth: Penguin Books, 1990).

REESE, G., 'Perspectives and Lacunae in Musicological Research', in B. S. Brook *et al.* (eds.), *Perspectives in Musicology* (New York: Norton, 1972).

RINK, J., Review of Berry, *Musical Structure and Performance* (1989), *Music Analysis*, 9/3 (1990), 319–39.

SACKS, O., *The Man who Mistook his Wife for a Hat* (London: Pan Books, 1986).

——*Seeing Voices* (Berkeley, Calif.: University of California Press, 1990).

SCHENK, H. G., *The Mind of the European Romantics* (London: Constable, 1966).

SCHENKER, H., *Beethovens neunte Sinfonie* (Vienna: Universal Edition, 1912).

SCHER, S. P. (ed.), *Music and Text: Critical Inquiries* (Cambridge: Cambridge University Press, 1992).

SCHERCHEN, H., *Handbook of Conducting*, trans. M. D. Calvocoressi (Oxford: Oxford University Press, 1993; first published 1933).

SCHOENBERG, A., *Style and Idea* (London: Faber and Faber, 1975).

SESSIONS, R., *The Musical Experience of Composer, Performer, Listener* (Princeton, NJ: Princeton University Press, 1971; first published 1950).

SLOBODA, J., *The Musical Mind: The Cognitive Psychology of Music* (Oxford: Oxford University Press, 1993, first published 1985).

STEIN, E., *Form and Performance* (London: Faber and Faber, 1962).

STORR, A., *Music and the Mind* (London: Harper Collins, 1992).

STRAUS, J. N., *Remaking the Past: Musical Modernism and the Influence of the Tonal Tradition* (Cambridge, Mass.: Harvard University Press, 1990).

STRAVINSKY, I., *Poetics of Music* (Cambridge, Mass.: Harvard University Press, 1942).

STRUNK, O., *Source Readings in Music History* (New York: Norton, 1950).

TARUSKIN, R., 'The Pastness of the Present', in N. Kenyon (ed.), *Authenticity and Early Music* (Oxford: Oxford University Press, 1988).

VALENTI, F., *A Performer's Guide to the Keyboard Partitas of J. S. Bach* (New Haven, Conn.: Yale University Press, 1989).

WALLIN, N. L., *Biomusicology: Neurophysiological, Neuropsychological and Evolutionary Perspectives on the Origins and Purposes of Music* (Stuyvesant, NY: Pendragon Press, 1991).

WARNOCK, M., *Imagination* (London: Faber and Faber, 1980; first published 1976).

WEBSTER, J., 'Analysis and the Performer, Introduction', *Early Music*, 20/4 (Nov. 1991).

WHITE, E. W., *Stravinsky: The Composer and his Works* (2nd edn., London: Faber and Faber, 1979).

WHITTALL, A., *Romantic Music* (London: Thames and Hudson, 1987).

WINTLE, C., 'Analysis and Performance: Webern's Concerto Op. 24/ii', *Music Analysis*, 1/1 (1982), 73–99.

WOLPERT, L., *The Unnatural Nature of Science* (London: Faber and Faber, 1992).

Index